J.B.Bradford.

BRIGADIER-GENERAL
R. B. BRADFORD, V.C., M.C.

AND

HIS BROTHERS.

"No one died with more glory, yet many died
and there was much glory."

First published just after the Great War for private circulation
among members and friends of the Bradford family.

This limited edition of 300 copies published by
Ray Westlake - Military Books
53 Claremont, Malpas, Newport, Gwent, South Wales.

Grateful thanks to Jonathan Leslie Bradford Cremer and his sons
Christopher, Andrew and Michael for providing the original
volume and permission to reprint.

Also thanks to Christina Boyd-Smith
who`s help and enthusiasm has been invaluable.

I.S.B.N. 1 871167 24 8

Copy number..31....

Printed by Antony Rowe Limited, Chippenham, Wiltshire

DEDICATION.

———

This Book is dedicated to the Memory of Three Brothers :—

Lieut.-Commander GEORGE NICHOLSON BRADFORD, v.c., Royal Navy, aged 31, who fell in Action on the Mole, Zeebrugge, April 23rd, 1918.

Lieutenant JAMES BARKER BRADFORD, M.C., The Durham Light Infantry, aged 27, who died in France, of wounds received in Action, May 14th, 1917.

Brig.-General ROLAND BOYS BRADFORD, v.c., M.C., The Durham Light Infantry, aged 25, who fell in Action in France, November 30th, 1917 ; and

TO ALL THOSE WHO WENT OUT TO FIGHT IN THE GREAT WAR AND DID NOT RETURN.

It is desired to thank all who helped in the preparation of this little book, but more especially to acknowledge the assistance given by C. Turley-Smith, M.A., and Major T. Welch, M.C.

CHAPTER I.

THE BRADFORDS come from what is called in the North of England "good Border stock." For generations they have been engaged in agriculture either in Northumberland or just across the Border.

A search might be made far and wide, and then made in vain, to find people more reticent and reserved than these Border families. They have always been fearless, and in the strenuous times through which they have lived they needed to be, for those of us who have only a nodding acquaintance with history know that life in the British Isles was not conspicuously peaceful in the seventeenth and eighteenth centuries, and nowhere was it more uncertain and vehement than in the Border country.

The books that have been handed down in the family give a clear insight into the characters of the Bradfords' forbears. These volumes consist chiefly of Bibles and of books dealing with religion and agriculture. Most of the religious books are of the stern, Puritan type, and no one can read or even glance at them without being warned of the extremely painful fate that awaits all sinners. If the most efficacious way to prevent sin is to exaggerate its penalties, these books are unreservedly to be recommended.

A tradition exists in the Bradford family that at one time they held estates at Bradford, a village near Bamburgh, Northumberland. The village is believed to have taken its name from the Bradfords, and to have been lost by them in one of those local but sanguinary fights which in the past frequently took place around the Border. If this tale is true, it would be exceedingly interesting to know the names of the warriors who succeeded in beating the Bradfords in a fight.

Another tradition, possibly more attractive and exciting to youthful minds, is that one of the Bradford ancestors was a famous Border cattle stealer, and gaily continued his adventurous career until he was captured and summarily hanged. No wonder that the young Bradfords of a later generation were especially interested in this reckless and romantic namesake when they read Wilson's *Tales of the Borders*.

Whatever may be true and whatever legendary in these traditions it is quite certain that George Bradford, the father of the four sons whose record in the Great War is so brilliant, came of a courageous and independent stock, and was himself a man of physical strength and of a character austere enough, but of an austerity that was always tempered by real affection for and pride in his children.

Born on March 21st, 1845, at Churnside, a village just on the Scottish side of the Border, George Bradford was educated in Northumberland and later at Houghton-le-Spring Grammar School, Co. Durham, and then served his time at the Earl of Durham's Lambton Collieries. After receiving his certificate as a Mining Engineer he became a Colliery Manager at the Lambton Collieries. Later he was appointed Manager of Messrs. H. Stobart's Bishop Auckland Collieries, and after staying there for some years he developed a small colliery of his own. Of great activity, he had by this time become interested in various enterprises. He was Chairman both of a

2

Steel Company near Darlington, and of the Newport Abercarn Collieries, in Wales, and he also visited and inspected coal properties in Canada and Spain.

After leaving Stobart's George Bradford went to live at a farm called Morton Palms, about four miles from Darlington, and four years later moved into Darlington itself; and there he spent the remainder of his life. It was during the years spent at Morton Palms that his children gained some of the physical health and strength with which they were exceptionally blessed.

With so many and so varied business interests to occupy his attention he had little time, and possibly less inclination, for anything resembling frivolity, but the love of sport was his by inheritance, and he shot and fished when opportunity came his way.

Rather late in life, in 1885, he married Amy Marion Andrews, a Kentish lady, whose gentle disposition and artistic and musical tastes were of infinite value in the Darlington home. Mr. Bradford died in 1911, aged 66.

The children of this marriage were:

Thomas Andrews Bradford, born 1886.
George Nicholson Bradford, born 1887.
James Barker Bradford, born 1889.
Roland Boys Bradford, born 1892.
Amy Isabelle Bradford, born 1901.

The boys' love for all sports was vigorous by the time their sister was born, and when Roland was told of her birth he at once remarked that it " would make the sides odd for games."

As the boys began to grow up their keenness upon outdoor life and games became more and more noticeable, and their father frequently took part in these games and encouraged them.

Self-contained as a family the Bradfords neither made many friends nor felt the need of them, but the children grew up with a genuine love for one another, a love which, it is true, was not demonstrative, but was none the less real because it was not conspicuously displayed.

From their childhood the young Bradfords were given far more liberty and freedom than is usually the lot of children in their station of life. Their father, being himself a man of independent mind, encouraged his children to do things for themselves and to depend neither on other people nor on circumstance. When the two elder boys were scarcely in double figures as regards age, they had on week days to walk four miles to Darlington Grammar School and four miles back, which is really rather a strenuous performance for small children in all weathers.

As a family the Bradfords had an excellent custom which played an important part in their lives. When the children were still very young Mr. and Mrs. Bradford began to read aloud to them, and presently the time came when the children themselves took more than a listening part in these readings. Such books as *Pilgrim's Progress, Robinson Crusoe,* and *Tom Brown's Schooldays* (in which book the famous fight made the boys eager to go to a public-school) were chosen, and the meanings of words not understood by the younger members of this reading party were carefully explained to them. Ample evidence is available to prove that this custom of reading aloud had a great influence upon the characters of the young Bradfords. "I am sure," one of this reading party has said, "that the reading aloud of all the best boys' books, in which the hero is such a gallant fellow and everything goes well with

4

him, had a most extraordinary effect on our characters. And this reading aloud by the family when we were at an impressionable age stamped high ideals into us while we were children."

At an early age the young Bradfords were also taught to learn and recite various poems of great deeds, and no one ever gave more spirited renderings of " Horatius " than they did.

Later on these reading parties dealt faithfully with Histories of the British Empire, Wilson's *Tales of the Borders,* Shakespeare, and Dickens (to whose work Mr. and Mrs. Bradford were especially devoted).

But fond as the Bradford children were of reading and being read to, it is to be doubted if any printed page delighted them as much as the tales Mr. George Andrews, their maternal grandfather, used to tell them.

Mr. Andrews was a sportsman in the best sense of that much-abused word, a man who could not fail to win the love and admiration of healthily-minded children. Although over seventy years of age when he visited Darlington, he used to put on the boxing gloves and instruct his grandchildren in the " noble art of self-defence." And it was no small honour to be instructed by him, for he had boxed with such renowned fighters as Tom Sayers and Jem Mace, and he had seen many of the great prize-fights, including the historic battle between Tom Sayers and Heenan.

Add to this that Mr. Andrews had a natural gift for story-telling, and then one can imagine how eagerly his visits to Darlington were looked forward to, and how clamorously his grandchildren besought him to tell those stories of pluck and endurance, which he told so dramatically and so well. Mr. Andrews had no small part in encouraging and stimulating the

5

Bradford boys to train themselves to become physically fit and strong and to avoid the dangers and temptations that destroy, or at any rate impair, both physical and mental health. And there is no doubt that they were naturally inclined to respond ardently to such teaching.

Their almost passionate devotion to games made them put as high a value on physical fitness as any professor of physical culture has ever placed upon it. They wanted to be strong and well so that they could enjoy their games and improve in them; and small blame to them. But they loved " the game beyond the prize." Indeed, prizes for games never entered their heads. " It did not matter whether we were good at them or not," one of them wrote, " it was the love of the game."

Games indeed formed a very definite part of the lives of the young Bradfords; their ambitions were for some years almost exclusively given up to them, and the reason is as clear as sunlight. For one of the dominant characteristics of the Bradfords was that they had to be persuaded that things were worth doing and having, before they devoted the whole of their energy to them. Games were worth doing, there was no doubt whatever in their minds about that, but school-work was altogether a different matter. It might lead to something, but what did it lead to? You had got to do it because there was trouble if you didn't. But it was permissible to do as little as possible, because it took time which might be given to more important matters!

No vision of double firsts at Oxford or Cambridge floated before the eyes of these boys; W. G. Grace was a greater hero to them than any scholar dead or living. The sound of a ball against a bat was the sweetest of all sounds, to hit a half-volley plumb in the middle of the bat was the most delightful of all sensations.

But when it is admitted that work in school did not appeal to the Bradford boys as urgently as games or any out-of-door sports, it would be far from the truth to say that they entirely neglected their school-work. Indeed, when they realised that work had got to be done so that an examination, which led to something definite, had got to be passed, they set to work with a persistent steadiness that was altogether admirable. Roland, who went to school at Epsom College, did not work hard while he was there, but as soon as he had made up his mind to enter the Army he worked with a determination that was all the more praiseworthy because up to that time he scarcely knew what work meant. But hard as he worked at that time he wrote to one of his brothers and said that he gave up a part of each day to exercise "so that I may keep myself fit." This desire to be physically fit always exercised a tremendous influence over the boys, and it was bred in them. Their forbears, both on their father's and mother's side, had been strong, healthy people, tall above the average, clean-living, clean-thinking men and women, and they bequeathed to the generation of which we are speaking an inheritance that all the gold in the world could not buy.

Looked at from the point of view of those who think that children should be pampered and never allowed to think or act for themselves, the upbringing of the Bradfords may seem to be more than a little strenuous. Their father believed in the rod, and did not spare it. But he was proud of his children and anxious that they should develop into fine people; and he was a man who could be loved as

7

well as feared, and under all and every condition he won respect and admiration.

Writing, after Lieut.-Com. George Bradford, V.C., R.N., had fallen in the attack on Zeebrugge, Vice-Admiral Sir William Goodenough, K.C.B., M.V.O., said: "A friend of mine knew Mr. Bradford, a more honest English gentleman never lived, so was his son in every spirit he possessed."

There may have been but little room for sentimentality in the Bradford home, but there was ample room for good, honest affection and sound common-sense. And in this healthy atmosphere the young Bradfords passed from childhood to boyhood, and from boyhood to early manhood, knowing well enough that the time would come when they had to rely upon their own efforts for a livelihood, but not in the least depressed by the fact.

"Good Border stock," than which there is none more sound in the world, and none that proved itself more dependable in years of crisis and danger.

CHAPTER II.

When war was declared in August, 1914, the Bradford brothers were as fit as men can be to take their part in it. Devoted as they had always been to games, they had never allowed them to become their masters. The Bradfords used games as a means to an end, and the end was to keep themselves in perfect health. It is true, but unimportant, that they happened thoroughly to enjoy the means.

In the years preceding 1914 even those of us with the shortest memories will recollect that we lived in a constant state of rumour as regards Germany's intentions towards us. On one side were people who were certain that Germany was steadily preparing and eagerly waiting for "the day." On the other side were men who were furious at what they called "alarmist reports circulated for political purposes." With either the one side or the other it was wise not to disagree, unless we wished to involve ourselves in an argument that was apt to be as heated as it was barren of result.

In the characters of the Bradfords was a solidity that prevented them from becoming unduly agitated by these rumours. With admirable directness they continued to mind their own business, and it was not their business to interpret or misrepresent Germany's intentions. But it was not only their business but also their duty to be ready for any call that their country might make upon them, and when that call came they were perfectly prepared to answer it.

Of the four brothers, Captain Thomas Andrews Bradford, D.S.O., is the only one who has survived the war, and he was wounded.

After being educated for some years at Darlington Grammar School, Captain Bradford went, when he was fourteen years old, to the Royal Naval College at Eltham. We have the best authority for saying that he was not specially studious at school, and the same excellent authority for stating that he worked hard after leaving Eltham.

When his school days were over he joined the 4th Volunteer Bn. D.L.I., and was transferred to the Territorials when they took the place of the Volunteer Force. In 1906 he received his commission in the 8th Battalion Durham Light Infantry, and received his second star in October of the same year. In 1910 he was promoted to a captaincy in the 8th (Territorial) Battalion D.L.I.

By profession a land-agent and farmer, Captain Bradford was also interested in collieries, and in these years of peace he won many honours in the world of sport.

He played forward for the Durham County XV., and as a cricketer his performances would have driven pessimism from the most despondent spectators. On several occasions he made a century for the Durham County XI., and even when he became captain of the side he did not allow his responsibilities to interfere with the power and frequency with which he hit the ball. But perhaps the performance that is best to remember in these days of careful cricket is one that stands to his credit in a Durham Senior League match. In this game he made 207, not out, in 90 minutes, a feat of which G. L. Jessop himself might reasonably be proud. There can be little doubt that had opportunity come his way he could have made a name for himself as a first-class cricketer.

In April, 1915, he went out to France with the 8th Batt. D.L.I. He was wounded at the second battle of Ypres, and later on he was mentioned in Despatches, and was awarded the D.S.O. Later he became Staff Captain and Brigade Major, and in 1917 he was given a permanent regular commission in the York and Lancaster Regiment.

In 1915 Captain Bradford married Honor Rebe, daughter of Colonel Blackett, C.B.E., D.L., and their son, born in 1920, has been called after each one of his gallant Bradford uncles. In October, 1922, Captain Bradford made a sporting effort to enter Parliament as a Conservative, and took part in a three-cornered contest in the Seaham Division of Durham. Mr. Sidney Webb was his Labour opponent, and at no time could the prospect of a Conservative victory be said to be bright. The figures of this election were :

Sidney Webb (Labour) 20,203
Capt. T. A. Bradford, D.S.O. (Con.) 8,315
Major E. Hayward (Lib.) 5,247

But, heavy as the majority was, Captain Bradford put up a plucky fight, and at least had the consolation of giving over 8,000 Conservatives a chance to use their votes.

Retaining his interest in politics, he again made a determined attempt to enter Parliament at the General Election in December, 1923. On this occasion he was the Conservative candidate for the Durham division of Co. Durham, and was defeated by a majority of 3,200.

Lieutenant - Commander George Nicholson Bradford, V.C., R.N., was born on April 23rd, 1887, at Witton Park, Durham, and was killed just 31 years later on a St. George's Day that will be remembered for all time in British History.

In an article which was published in the *Cornhill Magazine* in December, 1918, upon the Zeebrugge Attack, Lt.-Commander Hilton Young, D.S.C., wrote : " Bradford climbed up a davit and jumped ashore. He was the first man on the Mole. Hawkins, his second in command, climbed up by a line. The Mole at that point was swept by machine-gun fire and by rifle fire from snipers, and it was incessantly illuminated by star shells and rockets. They must have well known how desperate was their undertaking; there could not, I think, have been a braver act."

Thus George Bradford died, glorious in his death as he had been lovable and reliable in his life. Very quiet but always cheerful, his was a nature so sympathetic that he made many and lasting friends. Without any exaggeration it may be said that he had a real gift for friendship.

During his school-days, which were spent first at Darlington Grammar School, secondly at the Royal Naval College, Eltham, and finally at Eastman's, he worked harder than any of his brothers. He passed into the Navy 59th out of 77 successful candidates, and from that moment he energetically but unostentatiously applied himself to his profession. He was not ambitious, nor was he particularly keen upon promotion, but as one who knew him well has said of him, he " went steadily on."

But before the War broke out George Bradford was given a chance—which he promptly took—to show that he was the man for an emergency, even if he wished in the main to go " steadily on " and avoid the lime-light. On a dark March night the

Destroyer *Doon* rammed the trawler, *Halcyon*, and the following account of the collision has been written by an eye-witness:

" At 3.20 a.m. on Wednesday, March 3rd, H.M.S. *Doon* rammed the trawler, *Halcyon*, of Lowestoft, 15 miles east of the Owers Light. The *Doon* was proceeding to Dover to escort the King to Calais, and was accompanied by the *Chelmer*. The trawler was struck fair on the port side by the bow of the *Doon*. The latter was going at about 15 knots at the time, and the trawler at 8 knots. Five of the trawler's crew jumped on board the *Doon*, leaving four in the sinking ship. Searchlights were turned on by both the *Doon* and the *Chelmer*, but that of the *Chelmer* soon failed, and all the rescue work had to be done by the aid of the *Doon's* light.

" When the collision occurred the lifeboat of the *Chelmer* was called away, but, as it was turned in and covered ready for escort duty, some trouble ensued in getting it away, all the hitches of the cover jamming. The cook's knife and a few files were obtained and the cover was soon removed, and the boat lowered.

" About ten to fifteen minutes after the collision the *Chelmer's* whaler, in charge of Mr. Bradford, proceeded to the trawler and rescued three men. On the return of the whaler, the Captain of the *Chelmer* (Captain Loftus-Jones, who in the Great War received the V.C.) pulled over to the trawler, but considered that she was sinking rapidly, and therefore did not go on·board.

" The whaler again returned, and was about to be hoisted when a signal came from the *Doon* that there was a boy on board the sinking trawler. The whaler, containing the first lieutenant, Mr. Bradford, immediately pulled over to the fast sinking ship.

"Mr. Bradford sprang on board, rushed to the fore peak, now inky black, and as the trawler gave a lurch appeared with the unconscious boy in his arms. (The boy, who was coming up the hatch when the collision occurred, had been stunned by a fall.) The gallant officer arrived just in time, for as he jumped into the whaler the trawler up-ended, and her bow alone remained out of water. A few minutes later she sank.

"The *Chelmer* escorted the *Doon* back to Portsmouth. Luckily the *Doon's* collision bulkhead stood. Her bows were badly damaged."

Physical fitness was to George Bradford, as to all of his brothers, a necessity, and in every kind of sport, and especially in boxing, he was exceptionally successful. Additionally his sympathy with everyone who honestly tried to " do his job " helped him to become a splendid coach and trainer of any team or crew that was lucky enough to secure his services.

Prizes for boxing fell to him in great numbers, and his reputation as a skilled and determined boxer was firmly established in the Navy.

Writing to his sister in January, 1918, from H.M.S. *Orion,* he said: " I have just read an amusing passage in ' The Long Trick,' by Bartimeus, describing my (Lieut. Adams in the book) boxing bout with Seaman Hayes (Hands in book). Chapter ' Arma Virumque ' . . . ' Bartimeus ' is one Ricci, originally two terms above me, who went blind in one eye, and turned over to Paymaster."

The contest was held on Admiral Jellicoe's Flagship during the War, and, as anyone who knows the work of " Bartimeus " will expect, full justice is done to it.

"A Lieutenant-Commander," "Bartimeus" wrote, "appeared at the doorway from the smoking-room.

"'There will be an exhibition bout next,' he shouted, 'and then the final of the Light Weights.' A general move ensued on to the upper deck.

"The raised ring was in amidships before the after superstructure. The officers occupied tiers of chairs round three sides of the platform. The Admirals and their Staffs in front, and the Post-captains of the ships that had entered competitors, just behind. On the forward side, extending the whole breadth of the ship, was the dense array of the ship's company. . . . The judges were taking their seats at the little tables on either side of the ring, and the referee, an athletic-looking Commander, was leaning over from his chair talking to the Chaplain, who was acting as time-keeper.

"The Physical Training Officer of the Flag-ship stepped into the empty ring and raised his hand for silence. The hum of voices died away instantly, and in the stillness the thin, querulous crying of the gulls somewhere astern alone was audible.

"'Lieutenant Adams, Welter-Weight Cham-pion of the Navy, and Seaman Hands, ex-Middle-Weight Champion of England, have kindly con-sented to give an exhibition of sparring,' he proclaimed, and withdrew.

"During the applause that greeted the announcement a youthful figure, clad in a white singlet and football shorts, with a sweater thrown over his shoulders, ducked under the ropes and walked rather shyly to his corner of the ring. His appear-ance was the signal for a vociferous outburst of applause. . . . The clapping suddenly redoubled, and a broad, bull-necked man of about forty vaulted lightly into the ring and took his place in the opposite corner. He was stripped to the waist; his jaws moved mechanically about a piece of chewing gum, and an expression of benign good humour and enjoyment lit his battered, kindly countenance.

" It was not until the gong sounded and the two men rose from their chairs that the contrast between the toughened ex-professional and the lithe graceful amateur brought forth a little murmur of delight from the vast audience. . . .

" The Lieutenant was perhaps fifteen years the junior. . . . Deep-chested, lean-flanked, perfectly proportioned, and perhaps a shade ' fine-drawn '—England and America carelessly produce and maintain the standard of this perfection of physical beauty as no other white race can.

" The two men met in the centre of the ring, and as they shook hands the old pugilist grinned almost affectionately. . . .

" The two boxers had slipped into their habitual poses and were quietly moving round each other. The graceful activity of the amateur was somewhat characteristic of his school, while the ex-professional contented himself with almost imperceptible movements of his feet, watching with a nonchalant yet wary caution for the coming attack. With the suddenness of a flash the Lieutenant led with his left and was back out of harm's way again.

" True and quick was the blow, but the veteran's defence was even quicker. Without raising either glove he appeared to have swayed backwards from the hips. . . .

" Then for three short rounds there followed a completely enthralling display. On one side was perfectly trained orthodox amateur boxing. On the other every clean trick and subterfuge of irreproachable ring-craft. . . .

" In the last few seconds of the final round, however, a little out of breath with his defensive display, the older man changed his tactics. With lowered head and ferocious face he advanced, a whirling bulk of might and action, upon the amateur. Tap; tap; tap! Left-right, over and under, through the guard and round the guard of the outfought youngster the unclenched gloves totted up a score of points.

" There was a careful restraint behind each blow, yet, when the gong sounded and they smilingly shook hands amid tumults of enthusiasm, a thin red stream was trickling from the right eyebrow of the amateur champion.

" As they left the ring two boyish forms slipped through the ropes and made their way to their respective corners. . . . Both bore traces of previous conflicts upon their features, and their united ages aggregated something just over thirty."

Boxing was perhaps George Bradford's favourite sport of all sports. He not only excelled in it himself, but he also followed closely the careers of men who were professionals of the ring.

Writing to his sister, who was fourteen years his junior, in 1917, he said : " Hope the confirmation is going on all right; when asked why you want to be confirmed don't say as one of the boys at Eltham did, ' To get it over.' Yes, I saw that Wilde beat Symonds, I have seen the latter box. You are very observant to have noticed it."

As regards this Confirmation, another of the brothers gave his sister a piece of advice that was wonderfully comprehensive and characteristic of the family. " Never," he said, " do anything that you would be ashamed to tell your father and mother. And brush your teeth."

Much thought and eloquence might be spent over candidates for Confirmation without arriving at advice so simple and so sane.

This sanity which was characteristic of all the brothers was George Bradford's to a remarkable extent. He never talked about religion, he would have thought it arrogant if not actually improper to do so, but he lived it calmly and consistently. And the result was that his influence over both men and boys was enormous. They trusted and loved him.

Stimulated without doubt by the family-readings in which he had taken part as a boy, he was always a keen and discriminating reader. His favourite authors were Shakespeare and Dickens, but through the tensest years of the War he never lost his interest in modern fiction. And the letters which he wrote to his sister during this period reveal him both as a shrewd critic and adviser, whose advice was the more valuable because it was always flavoured by his quiet sense of humour.

" I apologise," he wrote, " for omitting to thank you for ' The Student in Arms,' it is very good. . . . Good luck to you at school, keep the Bradford name like that of Bayard, ' chevalier sans peur,' possibly mis-quoted but conveys the right idea. I think the war is going on well and the prospects excellent, don't allow anyone with a long face to say otherwise. This is my personal propaganda, and I am sure it is right."

And a letter which he wrote during March, 1917, is as fatherly as it is brotherly. " Jimmy " (the third brother) " has been doing very well, and I trust a grateful country may give him a decoration. I think he strongly deserves it for his all-round ability and most of all, tenacity, or in the homely, expressive, but unladylike phrase 'guts.' . . . Talking of . . . reminds me of those nauseating pictures in the . . . of Society ladies in toy Red Cross gear; there must be a lot of good in them though in spite of the foolish parading. Hope the foot is better. Look out that you walk on your boots and not over on one side only, like so many girls. Just notice if I am not right."

Writing again on the 1st of July, 1917, he shows how thoughtful he was of his mother. " You are quite right about the canoe, the stern is the place to steer from, only great men like me can do it from forward. I suppose you liked ' David Copperfield '; ' Dombey and Son ' is one of my favourites. You should give Mother an optimistic letter from time to time, she has been much shaken by her illness and Jimmy " (who died of wounds in May, 1917). " Weather here glorious, winning the war, in fact everything going splendidly. No aches, no pains, a pleasure to be alive."

Writing a month later he says : " *Moi,* I am a Lieut. Commander, having completed eight years as Lieut. . . . The *D. Mail* says that the Durhams have enhanced their fighting reputation in the recent offensive; I hope the Colonel (Roland) is all right and has done well." And then in a postscript he refers to a phrase that ran rampant over England and has not yet concluded its run. " What," he asks, " does ' simply priceless ' mean? You should try to preserve our beautiful old English language !" Towards the end of September in the same year he proved himself a true prophet. " I have just," he said, " read that school book ' *The Loom of Youth,*' by Alec Waugh, who was only 18 years old when he wrote it. It is V.G., but to me it seems somewhat precocious. How goes the war with you, does grub seem plentiful in the country? I think before we see the end it is going to test the endurance of all the fighting countries, not so much the actual soldier and sailor, but the civilians. Au revoir, keep cheerful, if only to encourage others, there is nothing like being a Mark Tapley."

All these letters, written from H.M.S. *Orion* to his sister, are signed " Your affect. brother G. N. Bradford," and in one which he wrote in November, 1917, he drew an arrow pointing at the initial " G " and added, " Curious thing, I have never written George in my life. A quaint family i' faith, pukka Dickens' characters."

Proud and fond of his family as George Bradford was, he never ceased to be good-naturedly amused by either their or his own peculiarities.

In the same month (November, 1917) he wrote : " The idea of you getting a sewing certificate amuses me, still it is V.G. work and ' even the ranks of Tuscany can scarce forbear to cheer.' I won't be able to come home for Xmas, but will doubtless be keeping the pot boiling in the North Sea, which will serve a good purpose. I think the Huns will have had all they want by this time next year. Still *qui vivra verra, moi qui vous parle* (you have surely noticed that people who are real duds at a language almost invariably quote it) *encore chacun à son goût* or something fairly near that."

And he concluded this brief excursion into French by asking his sister to cheer up their mother as much as possible. " She has done a lot for us, and at present leads a very lonely life."

Before he wrote again Roland Bradford had been killed. " Poor old Roland will live in history, a marvellous leader of men and died a glorious death."

Early in 1918 George Bradford left the *Orion* to prepare for the Zeebrugge operations, and in March he wrote from H.M.S. *Hindustan* : " The above is my address till I tell you otherwise. I shall go back to the *Orion* later on probably, as my present is only a temporary job."

Thus he refers casually to the attack on Zeebrugge, which was to cost him his life and at the same time to give him undying fame.

Continuing in the same letter he said : " T.A.B. (his eldest brother) and I stopped one night together at the Berners Hotel, and went to see ' The Bing Boys on Broadway.' We enjoyed it, but came to the conclusion that our artistic senses are not very strongly developed. . . You should read Julius Cæsar, Macbeth, Hamlet, Coriolanus, T. of Athens, Henry IV., V., VI., R. & Juliet at your leisure. They are extraordinarily good."

Writing again from the *Hindustan* at the beginning of April he said :

" I think you would make an excellent nurse and hope you get the chance. . . . There are some very good verses in the present ' Punch ' by O.S., who always seems to me to write sense. . . . The fighting in France must now be terrific, our civilian population always appear to be best when we are up against it. The Paris bombardment is just the theatrical business that appeals to the German mind. Confound their devices. I like the ship and my work very much."

And then a few days later came the last letter which his sister received from him. During the whole war he had been collecting Naval crests for her, and he rarely sent a letter without adding to her collection.

"Herewith a few crests," he wrote in this most characteristic letter, "I see you are doing well at School, the Bradfords are all clever, fate I suppose! Happy returns next month; '2 in May,' as you used to say. Au revoir, don't forget the Chevalier Bayard, *sans reproche,* etc. Best love, your affec. brother, G. N. Bradford."

Before "2 in May" George Bradford was dead, and the chorus of praise that he won, not only for his death most glorious but also for his wonderfully sympathetic, helpful and trustworthy life, has the genuine note that can be neither mistaken nor misinterpreted.

CHAPTER III.

The attack on Zeebrugge, so carefully planned and so brilliantly carried out, cannot fail to be recorded in history as one of the most magnificent exploits of the British Navy.

Of this wonderful achievement Marshal Foch, writing in appreciation of Captain Carpenter's book, *The Blocking of Zeebrugge*, says:

" C'est dans un sentiment de solidarité que s'est realisée l'union des Alliés, en 1914, quand la cause de la Civilisation s'est trouvée menacée.

" A tous les moments critiques de la guerre, l'union s'est ainsi resserrée devant le danger, et lorsqu'il s'est agi de fermer un des repaires d'où les sous-marins ennemis menaçaient les communications vitales des Alliés, dans une manœuvre splendide, avec un esprit commun de sacrifice absolu, le port de Zeebrugge a été attaqué et définitivement fermé.

" Le Commandant du *Vindictive* a tenu à rappeler les détails de l'opération dans laquelle il a joué un rôle si brillant, et son livre constituera un précieux enseignment et donnera aux générations futures un exemple splendide. " F. FOCH."

No one, indeed, can deny that such an action required " sacrifice absolu," and although, when compared with the gigantic losses suffered in some of the battles of the war, our losses at Zeebrugge may be considered small in quantity, our loss in quality was more than severe. For it is only just to say that the world has never known braver men than those who laid down their lives in this attack.

The two youngest of the Bradford brothers, James and Roland, were already killed, and it was heart-rending to be compelled to inform their mother that yet another of her sons was dead.

What consolation could be gained from sympathy, and from tributes of respect for her sailor-son, was abundantly hers. Nevertheless, Mrs. Bradford had a heavy burden to bear, and nobly she bore it.

Almost at once Captain Carpenter, V.C., R.N., wrote to George's brother, Captain Bradford, a letter that could not fail to be comforting :

" One may search historical records in vain to find any instance of more splendid gallantry than that shown by George Bradford.

" His supreme contempt for danger and his unforgettable self-sacrifice were typical, not only of those whose deeds gave birth to our traditions, but of himself. George Bradford was not only a great fighter but a great gentleman, a great friend and a great sportsman. His was a most lovable nature. Both in his everyday life and in the manner of his death he has set the rest of us an example of incalculable benefit. I feel that I can speak for my officers and men in *Vindictive* while recording here our pride at having known and served with your extremely gallant brother."

And in Captain Carpenter's excellent book, *The Blocking of Zeebrugge,* to which reference has previously been made, he describes the action off the Mole.

" *Iris,*" he says, " had reached the Mole and dropped her anchor at the foot of the wall, about 12.15 a.m., her position being roughly 100 yards ahead, i.e., to the westward, of *Vindictive*. The heavy swell was tossing her about like a cork, with

24

the result that the use of parapet anchors was extremely difficult. After several failures to get these parapet anchors hooked to the top of the wall Lieut. Claude E. K. Hawkings, one of the officers of the storming party, ordered some men to hold up one of the scaling ladders.

" They could not actually lean it against the wall; the rough nature of the latter and the surging of the ship would have combined to break the ladder immediately. The ladder was, therefore, merely sloping towards the wall without any support at its upper end. Hawkings ran up it and leaped to the top of the Mole, the ladder being smashed to pieces a moment later. He sat astride the wall for the purpose of fixing an anchor and appears to have been immediately attacked by some enemy on the parapet itself.

" He was seen defending himself with his revolver before he was actually killed. It was terribly sad that his great act should have cost him his life.

" Lieut.-Commander George N. Bradford, who was actually in command of the storming party in *Iris*, and whose duties did not include that of securing the ship, climbed up the ship's derrick which carried a large parapet anchor and which was rigged out over the Mole side of the ship.

" The derrick itself was crashing on the Mole with each movement of the ship, which, in turn, was rolling and pitching heavily; a more perilous climb can scarcely be imagined.

" Waiting his opportunity Bradford chose the right moment and jumped to the wall, taking the anchor with him. He placed the latter in position, but almost immediately was riddled with machine-gun bullets, and fell into the sea between *Iris* and the Mole. Gallant attempts were made to rescue his body, but owing to the darkness and the rush of the strong tidal stream he was swept beyond recovery.

" Nothing could have been finer than Bradford's efforts to secure the ship. He had been a splendid fighter in the ' ring '; it was against his nature to give in as long as there was the remotest chance of winning through; his death brought us a great loss of a great gentleman. Really, one cannot conceive greater bravery than was shown by these two officers, who have set an example which will surely never be forgotten."

Even in an age when memories are notoriously short it is inconceivable that these magnificent exploits will not always be remembered with pride.

" Few incidents of the Great War," Rear-Admiral Sims wrote, " had a greater influence in inspiring enthusiasm in the allied fighting forces and increasing their *morale* than the successful attack upon Zeebrugge." And with equal truth he might have added that no incident brought so clearly home to the Germans the hopelessness of the task on which they were engaged.

Admiral Viscount Jellicoe, G.C.B., O.M., G.C.V.O., was among the first to send to Mrs. Bradford his tribute of admiration for the heroism which her son had shown in the Zeebrugge attack.

" I remember your son so well, and admired his character as much as his great personal ability; the Service and the Country have indeed lost in him one who could ill be spared. He died, as one would have expected him to die, under circumstances of the greatest gallantry and with supreme self-sacrifice. From one who is very proud to have had so gallant an officer and so perfect a gentleman under his command."

Not once but repeatedly did those who had known George Bradford testify to the influence his character had over men and boys alike.

" George Bradford," Vice-Admiral Sir William Goodenough, K.C.B., M.V.O., wrote, " has not lived in vain, quite apart from the gallant act in which he met his death. He irradiated an influence that must make a great difference to many whether they knew it or not. Truth, Honour and Duty were instinctive and unconscious with him, and his firm mind moulded for many a shape and aspect of life that will remain with them always. And with it he combined a simplicity of friendship that made all love him."

Testimonies to the inspiration derived from George Bradford's life and death could, if it were necessary, be abundantly quoted. Here, however, only extracts from letters written by those who had exceptional opportunities to know him in his daily life are given.

Captain Fullerton, C.B., D.S.O., who commanded the *Orion*, wrote :

" I can truly say a more honourable, straight, and gallant English gentleman never lived, and his loss is not only great to us, his shipmates, but also a loss to the country and the world. He was beloved by all. . . . I have no doubt you know that your son was picked out from the whole of the 2nd Battle Squadron to command our men."

The Chaplain in the *Orion* lost a loved and valued friend when George Bradford was killed, and in words that are as sincere as they are touching he speaks of his and his shipmates' admiration and grief.

27

" He was so magnificent, so firm and patient and kind that we all, both officers and men, looked to him for guidance and advice. . . . The news of his death in the amazingly gallant attack on the German forts came as a great sorrow to every man in the ship. I was besieged wherever I went that morning with inquiries whether the report of his death were true. . . .

" The Boys, who were George's special care in the *Orion,* naturally loved him. ' He always had a smile for us,' one of them told me the other day, a description of himself which would have amused George, who used laughingly to say he was growing too serious.

" For myself, I like to think of George as he knelt among the men at communion; he would be there every alternate Sunday, and I am sure that his presence, because of his whole life, was a source of encouragement to many weaker ones, as it was a continual inspiration to myself."

More than once in writing to his sister George Bradford had referred to " *le Chevalier sans peur et sans reproche,*" so the letter written by Captain Dreyer, C.B., C.B.E., was especially happy :

" The world is the better for his having lived in it, and all of us who knew him are particularly conscious of this; his noble end is characteristic of his whole life.

" I can imagine him climbing the derrick and jumping on the Mole and securing the hawser, in which process he gave his life for his country and for his comrades on the *Iris,* who were waiting under fire for their ship to be secured to enable them to land.

" I shall always think of your son as ' *le Chevalier sans peur et sans reproche.*' "

28

In March, 1919, Mrs. Bradford, George's mother, received the following letter from Vice-Admiral Sir Roger Keyes, Bt., K.C.B., K.C.V.O., C.M.G., D.S.O.:

" Dear Mrs. Bradford,

" You wrote to me from Halstow Vicarage so I hope this will be forwarded without delay; but you may hear before my letter reaches you that your very gallant son, George, has been awarded the posthumous Victoria Cross which he so heroically earned on his birthday.

" I *knew* he would eventually get it, because although many actions were performed on that night by officers and men who survived, and by others who gave their lives, amongst the latter your son's act of glorious self-sacrifice stood out, I thought, alone. It will be a very great satisfaction to the many in the Service, who loved him and knew his worth, that he should have been selected with one other to repre-sent the gallant throng who did not survive.

" I know how deeply you have suffered in this war, but to have been the mother of such splendid sons must be some consolation to you. In all sympathy,

" I am, yours sincerely,

" Roger Keyes."

This gracious letter was dated March 14, and three days later Mrs. Bradford received a telegram from the Admiralty:

" Have much pleasure in informing you that the King has approved the posthumous award of the Victoria Cross to your son the late Lieut.-Cdr. George Bradford."

Writing of the Zeebrugge attack Lt.-Com-mander E. Hilton Young said: " There were many there whose names will not be forgotten; to have known them, even for a few short weeks, was as good a gift as life could give." And then referring to George Bradford he wrote that his manner " had ever the graciousness and gentleness with which the true warrior spirit is wont to surround itself, to save it from hurting other spirits less finely tempered than itself."

It was because George Bradford was throughout his life both supremely fearless and also consistently thoughtful of others that his loss was such a heavy blow to all who knew him. Of him it has been said with truth that he was a gallant sailor, a charming companion, and a loyal friend.

His body, which was cast up by the sea at Blankenberghe in Belgium some days after he was killed on the Mole, was buried in Blankenberghe communal cemetery by the Germans.

CHAPTER IV.

James Barker Bradford, the third of the brothers, was born at Witton Park, Co. Durham, on December 11, 1889, and died on May 14, 1917, aged twenty-seven, from wounds received in France.

He was educated at Darlington Grammar School and Polam Grange School, Darlington, and although it has been said of him that " he was not clever, but a plodder," he had one gift that had not been vouchsafed to his brothers. Roland Bradford, although almost passionately fond of music, was during his boyhood heard to produce sounds that made those who had to listen to them suspect that his gift for music was not as great as his enthusiasm. James Bradford and his sister were really musical.

Over six feet in height and strong and wiry, James took part in nearly every branch of sport with true Bradford zest; indeed his physique was one that any athlete might have envied. A fair cricketer and " soccer " player, he was also a good boxer, wrestler and swimmer, and additionally he hunted with the Hurworth Hounds.

With his most generous disposition and simple faith in the honesty of all the world James Bradford was a man for whom it was impossible not to feel a warm affection. His sympathetic outlook upon life, and his quickness to see points of view that were not his own made him exceptionally successful in handling men.

After leaving school he served his time at Hawthorn Leslie's Engineering Works, Newcastleon-Tyne, as an Engineer, and later on became a Director of the Dinsdale Wire and Steel Works, Co. Durham. For three years before the war he was in the Naval Reserve as an Able Seaman, and in 1913 he became a trooper in the Northumberland Hussars, and in 1914 he went out with them to France.

But before the war broke out, though the war-fever had begun to spread, James had done excellent recruiting work.

" When the great recruiting time was on," his sister has written, " Jimmie got lots of recruits for the Yeomanry. Many of them were men who had never been on a horse, and he used to teach them to ride and jump in the garden on Sundays, on his mare Kitty and my pony."

As a trooper in the Northumberland Hussars James was perfectly contented and happy. He had never been an officer, and he had no ambition to become one. Consequently a lot of persuasion and argument was required before he could be induced to change his mind. In 1915, however, he yielded to the persuasions of his brother Roland, who told him that he would be of more value as an officer. Soon afterwards he was given a Commission in the 18th Battalion, the Durham Light Infantry (Kitchener's Army).

During the summer of 1916 James married Miss Annie Wall, of Darlington; no child resulted from this marriage.

On August 1, 1916, he was wounded on the Somme, the official description of his wound being " G.S.W. arm and right ankle." In consequence of this wound he spent several months in England, but early in 1917 he was back again on the Somme, and on April 17, the *London Gazette* contained the following notice :—

" Awarded the Military Cross.

———

" Temp. 2nd Lieutenant James Barker Bradford, 18th Bn. Durham Light Infantry.

" For conspicuous gallantry and devotion to duty. He gallantly led his men into the enemy's trench, capturing many prisoners and two machine guns. He himself killed three of the enemy. Later he succeeded in repelling a determined enemy counter attack.

"(Hebuterne Sector, 3rd March, 1917.")

———

During that month of March George Bradford had expressed his hopes that " a grateful country would give Jimmy a decoration." And in the light of future events it is more than pleasing to think of George's gratification in, the fact that his brother's gallantry was so quickly recognised.

On the 10th of May, 1917, James was wounded again.

" G.S.W. left shoulder and left thigh," and from these wounds he died four days later. He was buried in Duisan's British Cemetery, near Arras, France, the first of the Bradford brothers to lay down his life for a cause in which he steadfastly believed and for a country which he dearly loved.

———

CHAPTER V.

Roland Boys Bradford, the youngest of the brothers, was born at Witton Park, Co. Durham, on February 22, 1892. When, on November 30, 1917, at the age of twenty-five, he was killed in France he had reached the rank of Brigadier-General and had been awarded the Victoria Cross and the Military Cross, and this statement proves beyond any question that Roland was a soldier of real genius, and also an exceptionally fearless man. To be the youngest of several brothers is not always an enviable position. Families have been known in which the youngest son has been petted by his parents, and consequently his brothers have considered that a little suppression would be beneficial. In the Bradford family, however, there was neither pampering nor petting, but there was a wholesome affection and a broad point of view.

We are told, for instance, that except when the children were quite young they were never *compelled* to go to church. To some people this free and easy way of regarding religious observances may seem to be a vast mistake, but however deeply it may shock those who think that a child who goes to church reluctantly is being given a sounder training than one who is allowed free choice in the matter, there is no gainsaying that as regards the Bradford children their parents' policy was more than justified. Religion remained an influence in all their lives, and we have abundant evidence to prove that during the years of war Roland was strongly impressed by its comfort and its power.

" I think," one who knew Roland very well has written, " that after he had been in the war for some little time he became most deeply impressed with the righteousness of our cause, and this combined with the fact that he was himself facing death, and seeing death around him every day, inspired him, and made him believe, like Cromwell, that it was a holy war. Also deep in his blood was the old Border Covenanting fervour inherited from his Border ancestors."

In 1898 the Bradfords moved into Darlington, and in the Quaker town Roland began his education at Queen Elizabeth's Grammar School. Afterwards he went to a private school, Polam Grange, and in May, 1907, he went to Epsom College, where he remained for three years.

Resembling his brothers in his devotion to games and, it must be admitted, his lack of zeal for work in school, he was different from them in one respect. To a remarkable extent he had been endowed with the gift of imagination, a gift that his brothers knew that they had missed. " Roland had," one of them has said, " far more brains than any of our family, and he was very vivacious, and we others were not."

That Roland had his own way of looking at things is shown by his remark, already mentioned, that his sister's birth, in 1901, would make " the sides odd for games." During the short nine years which he had lived he had become accustomed to his eldest brother and himself taking sides against George and James, and anything that was likely to upset such an admirable arrangement seemed to him at least to have grave inconveniences attached to it.

As a child, and later on as a boy, it is good to know that he was not without the spirit of mischief.

When quite a small boy he was sitting with his mother when a lady, who had come to call, was suddenly announced. Before the lady appeared in the room Roland was under a table and completely hidden from view. It was a situation that had to be dealt with promptly or not at all, and before Mrs. Bradford could make up her mind to extract Roland from his hiding-place her visitor was seated and talking with considerable rapidity. It is, however, to be supposed that Mrs. Bradford was a little distraught during this visit, for she was wondering all the time whether something might not be said that was at best scarcely suitable for youthful ears. Roland, however, was sufficiently punished for his sudden dive because he had to remain in his hiding-place during half-an-hour or more without having anything whatever to do except to keep quiet, a way of passing time which neither then nor later appealed to him in the smallest degree.

Later on when he had forgiven his sister for being born and had become very devoted to her, it is only the truth to say that his devotion occasionally displayed itself in ways that must have been more than a little exasperating.

" Roland," his sister has written, " was a tremendous tease, and he used to invent lurid crimes that my dolls had committed, and then he sentenced them to death and either hanged them or chopped off their heads. He generally made up for the damage he had done, and once when he went to Darlington Fair he bought heaps of things and put them into my stocking. He could carry ' Let's pretend ' to any lengths. But although he was extraordinarily imaginative he could also be absolutely matter-of-fact."

More casual as a boy and more happy-go-lucky than any of his brothers, Roland undoubtedly was. But although his young nature seemed to demand that his imagination should occasionally enjoy almost riotous freedom, he was also in some ways thoroughly practical. For instance, while still in his early teens, he arrived at the curious conclusion for a boy that " the inarticulate person " was useless to himself and everyone else. Fortified by this belief he took infinite trouble in learning to speak and to recite, and he used to shut himself in his room and declaim long passages of Shakespeare and French poetry. This training resulted in his becoming a fluent and eloquent speaker, and during the War his addresses to his men were both excellently worded and delivered. He was equally industrious in trying to become a musician, and he did succeed in learning to play one or two instruments. But the family verdict upon his musical ability is unfavourable. " No good at music but very keen. He taught himself to play the flute and mouth-organ (both badly)." And against this verdict no one is likely to appeal.

Roland could scarcely have been a Bradford if he had not taken an active part in sport and games. He played cricket fairly well, and at Epsom he was captain of his house football XV., and in his last year was in the College XV. as a forward.

At Epsom, however, his chief interest was given to the Cadet Corps, in which he became a section-commander. If at this time he had a leaning towards any profession it was towards the medical, but it is at least possible that the first seeds of his ultimate decision to become a soldier were sown while he was in the Cadet Corps at Epsom.

" I remember him," Mr. Lee, his housemaster at Epsom, has written, " as a bright, dark-eyed boy. He was never very prominent at work, and left us in the matriculation form. He was keen on fun and not above a practical joke, especially on the school sergeant at the store tent down at camp, but he was never really a troublesome boy."

No expectation that Roland would bring fame and unending inspiration to his school seems to have been entertained by the authorities at Epsom. But for this Roland himself was largely responsible. In later years he often deplored his idleness at school, but whatever he did not learn while at Epsom he certainly did learn some lessons that can be taught most admirably at our public-schools. Nor is he by any means the only boy who has been almost undistinguished during his school life, and then in later years has added undeniably to the glory of his school's record.

In addition to cricket and football Roland played hockey well and was a good swimmer, high diver and boxer. He was also a very keen fisherman, and was fond of long country walks with or without a companion.

When he left school, he was six feet in height, built on the lines of an athlete, and very good-looking. But although his family never had the smallest doubt that he would ultimately make a success of his life he had not yet made up his mind about the profession he wished to follow. For some little time he seemed to be content to fish and amuse himself, and his father naturally became anxious that the period of indecision should not be indefinitely prolonged. Then for several weeks Roland was fascinated by the idea of becoming a doctor, and so keen was he upon various experiments that his presence was not entirely without inconveniences. For Roland used to commandeer the breakfast-room, and there he carried on his scientific research with an ardour which those of the family who were living at home failed rather conspicuously to share. It is possible now to smile at the keenness with which he carried on these experiments, but it is only fair to add that at the time he was in grim earnest about them and that the energy with which he set to work showed that no real fears about his future need be felt.

Soon after leaving school Roland became an officer in the Church Lads' Brigade which was attached to Holy Trinity Church, Darlington, and in 1912 he acted as Adjutant to a Battalion at the annual sea-side camp.

" It was," a friend of his has written, " typical of his keenness and of his rigid insistence upon the priority of Duty that after being summoned home by telegram on account of his father's serious illness, he returned to the camp to finish his work."

Darlington is the Headquarters of the 5th Battalion of the Durham Light Infantry, and in April, 1910, Roland was appointed a 2nd Lieutenant to the local Territorial Company.

He was twice under canvas with his men; in July, 1910, at Richmond, a Brigade Camp, and in July, 1911, at Featherstone Park, Haltwhistle, a Divisional Camp; on both occasions his efficiency and keenness won warm praise from his commanding officers.

At Richmond he was so conspicuously excellent at the morning Physical Drill that Captain Ensor soon placed him in sole charge of it. Thus he got an opportunity to introduce several novelties into the movements, all of which were acknowledged to be successful. At Featherstone Park he acted as A.D.C. to Colonel Bush and rode " a fidgety roan mare which he managed jolly well, although she nearly ran away with him."

From his childhood Roland was fond of all animals, and directly the opportunities came his way he became a good horseman. And that he was the right kind of man to own a horse we know from the fact that whenever he was able he liked to feed and look after it himself.

After the second of these Territorial Camps Roland went for a month's course to a Regular Battalion—the 2nd Battalion, the Durham Light Infantry—at Colchester. It was, in Captain Bradford's opinion, the Church Lads' Brigade and the Territorials which made Roland incline towards a military career, "and the month's attachment to a Regular Battalion determined his choice for the Army." At any rate he soon gave up the idea of becoming a doctor, and the breakfast-room in the Darlington home was no more invaded for experimental purposes.

Roland's mind was definitely made up, and from that moment he worked with steady perseverance and concentration. "It was his first effort at real work, and he worked very hard."

Soon after joining the Special Reserve we find him with an Army Crammer in London, and in the summer of 1911 we hear that he was making "slow but sure progress with military work." In March, 1912, he passed the examination for a Commission in the Regular Army, his place being sixth among thirty-six successful candidates. In the following May he was gazetted as 2nd Lieutenant to the 2nd Battalion of the Durham Light Infantry.

CHAPTER VI.

Before leaving Roland Bradford's boyhood behind us it is excusable to look back at it and try to throw a clearer light upon a character that was unusually complex. For it is no exaggeration to say that Roland, as a boy, was not always easy to understand. He was both exceptionally imaginative and casual, and he was also equally practical and matter of fact. When his imagination was enjoying one of its outbursts, it is quite easy to believe that he astonished those who had, until then, seen only the practical side of his nature.

" I never," one of his brothers wrote, " saw him lose his temper, but he had a very quick tongue, and was very fond of arguing. He disliked being suppressed on account of his youth, and would never quit an argument with his elders for this reason, and he would stick to his opinions."

Now, we all know what an argumentative boy who refuses to be silenced is often, and justifiably, called. We call him either a great nuisance or a young prig, and more often than not we are right. But all the same we should be entirely wrong if we ever thought of applying these descriptions to Roland. And the reason of this is that he was born with a gift that all prigs are notoriously without, and this gift was undeniable charm of manner.

Add to this that he was almost as alive as his brother George to the funny side of himself and of his family, and we begin to see why Roland was never in danger of being thought a prig; though it is a fact that before the War he used to write long and rather pedantic letters, and while cutting—so to speak—his wisdom teeth, went through a phase that was not without its symptoms of priggishness.

Really this phase was due, and Roland himself frankly admitted it, to a real desire to find and to express himself. When a boy he kept a large note-book, which if without any real value in the literary sense, shows nevertheless how varied were his interests and what trouble he took to put his ideas clearly and forcibly upon paper.

We are told that his ideas were always original, and certainly the heading of this note-book is as original as it is delightful. It is called " Scraps of Roland Bradford when a Schoolboy." And the sub-title is " My Pigeons. Their Pedigrees, and other things about them." On the first page is written in an excellent hand for a boy of fourteen :

"Contents and Index."
A. The Huddersfield Pair.
B. H.C. Cock, and broken-winged hen.

Although this book was destined to contain many of Roland's earlier literary productions, the Index has to rest content with these two entries.

But as regards his pigeons Roland made a record, which is as illuminating about himself as it is about his birds.

It begins : " Flying Homers. The Huddersfield Pair. Cock, 13 months. Hen, 15 months. (June 3rd, 1906.) Bred. First egg, Jan. 20th. 2nd egg, Feb. 1st, 1906. Both of them hatched out (Feb. 18th, 1906) but did not live, at least only one did (the cock). I think the cat got it (the other). It was a great loss and a damper to me. Like a fool I omitted to ring them."

"Damper" indeed as this loss must have been to him it did not prevent him from continuing his record faithfully for a year. He concludes this account of his first effort at pigeon-breeding with : "The following lines of Shakespeare's are worthy of the hen : ' Age cannot wither her, nor custom stale her infinite variety.' Total at close of season, 8 eggs. 2 birds lived."

In this carefully written account of his pigeons, an account in which the cat appears over and over again as the villain of the piece, is one very characteristic entry. "Unluckily they again laid; I shall not allow them to hatch. I shall fly them both (the pair) every day to improve their condition."

It is easily to be imagined that to belong to Roland's small stud of pigeons was to know everything there was to be known about a strenuous existence. Physical fitness was already to him one of the most important things in life; belonging to the Bradford family it could hardly have been otherwise. And later on his note-book contains, in addition to some accounts of camps and a lurid story about stolen letters and blackmail, several articles dealing with physical culture. Some of these articles were published in *Health and Strength* and other papers, and they show clearly enough how eager Roland was that others should be as fit as he was, and also prove that his attempts to express himself only required practice to become successful.

For instance, the article on "Neck Exercises," from which quotations are given, gets to the point with a directness altogether admirable.

"The neck is a part of the body which Physical Culturists often overlook. It is quite common to see a well developed body attached to the head by a thin and weedy neck. A bull neck is still more unsightly, but a neck obtained by physical exercise is shapely and handsome. As the neck gets very little freedom, being encased in a stiff collar during the day—I think it of special importance that it should receive exercise.

" I give below the best exercises for producing a shapely and muscular neck."

He then proceeds to mention these exercises, and his instructions are plainly stated and easy to understand.

Another article begins : " I would like to call the attention of my readers to the value of ' Trunk Bending.' . . . It assures a firm and graceful carriage of the body and braces the whole system. A friend of mine, who had rather a large corporation, reduced his weight by a stone in one month by ' Trunk Bending.' " Again some excellent advice follows.

A short essay on Physical Culture for Boys was to be expected from Roland. But some of us may be a little astonished to find his interests were so embracing that he extended them to ladies. Articles in this note-book are to be found entitled, " Are Stays a Necessity?" and " How to maintain the complexion." With delicious gravity this second article begins, " This is a question which confronts every woman," and who is prepared to deny it?

It is easy enough now to smile good-naturedly at Roland Bradford settling down to write upon such subjects. But even as we smile we have got to remember that uppermost in his mind when he wrote these articles was the practice they gave him in self-expression. They were a part, and an important part, in a rigorous training of his mind, and they bore excellent fruit, as many a man who served under him in France can testify.

One who knew Roland very well and loved him very dearly has written : " He never did any work at school, but when he left school and realised at about 18 years of age that he had his own living to earn he soon changed. I think he reasoned it out as a business proposition : ' The sooner I start work the sooner will I be my own master.' At first he thought he would be a doctor, but very soon he changed to the Army. I think ambition played a large part in Roland's life, *but only in the beginning* of the War. I am certain that later on he had no thought about his career or himself. He looked upon it as a Holy War."

Just at one time Roland had an idea that he would like to enter Parliament, and during elections he loved to attend meetings and ask questions. This idea vanished into the back of beyond as soon as he had definitely chosen the Army as his profession, but it is all the same quite easy to believe that it would have come to life again if the War had spared him.

He was always a great reader, Dickens was one of his favourite authors, but as soon as he had decided to join the Army his reading was devoted more to Military History than to fiction, and he studied the history of the Boer War with profound interest and care. " He was delighted," it has been said, " to meet either officers or men who had served in South Africa, for each one of them could add something to his knowledge of the campaign. His conversation showed that he had a more than ordinarily intelligent grasp of the problems raised, settled or left behind by the South African War."

One more interest of Roland's in his earlier years remains to be mentioned, and that is cookery. Often when at home he would experiment in the making of cakes and puddings, and when in camp he kept an attentive eye upon the messing arrangements. During the years that he was preparing for the Army he worked steadily and systematically at languages, and when the day came for him to go to France he could talk the language of the country very fairly well. And everyone who was in France at any time during the War knows how valuable it was to be able to talk to our Allies in their own tongue.

It is not reasonable to suppose that anyone, when Roland joined the Army, expected him to have such a brilliant career as he had. For one thing, although there were rumours of war in 1912, our country was more distracted by internal troubles than by external enemies. And it is quite obvious that Roland could not have sprung so rapidly to fame in days of peace. He, like everyone else, needed his opportunity, but when it came to him one cannot imagine a man more fit in body and in mind to make the most of it. But although Roland lived the best years of his young life in times of war, it is clear enough that he had no sooner joined the Army than he impressed his senior officers with the idea that he was a subaltern of exceptional gifts. Captain F. G. Maughan has contributed the following account of Roland's early military career, and so great is its value that it is quoted in full :

" From the day that Bradford joined the Battalion I was conscious of his strong personality, and I think that others received the same impression. At the time we should not have expressed this in so many words, one did not stop to consider whether a newly-joined subaltern was gifted with a personality or not, but merely formed a general opinion whether he was the right material for making a useful soldier, whether he was likely to be a credit to the Army and his regiment.

46

" There were no two opinions about this as regards Bradford. From the beginning he was all keenness and enthusiasm in the right direction. He was ready to turn his hand to anything, no matter how unfamiliar the task might be, and he would set to work with a calmness and often an originality of thought which brought success, when older men did not expect that he would do more than make a good attempt.

" An eye was kept on newly-joined subalterns with a view to ensuring that if they had any money to spend, it was put to a more useful purpose than riotous living. In this connection all were encouraged to keep a horse and to hunt if this was within their means. Bradford had probably not had great experience of horses before joining, but he took to hunting with enthusiasm, went well, and was ever ready to learn all he could.

" The result showed itself in a striking manner at Lichfield in the Spring, of 1914. As the hunting season drew to an end, Bradford, without seeking advice, bought a horse at a price which, I understood, must have required some nerve. He entered it in a local point-to-point, and though he had no previous experience of riding in a point-to-point, he won a fine race and in good company.

" He took a prominent part in all games, especially in those with his men, organising them and leading them, but never interfering in the rôle of an officer in a manner to mar the men's enjoyment. Indeed, both in and out of work his relations with his men were in accordance with the best traditions of the old Army.

" His activities were not confined to pursuits which appeal naturally to an athletic lad of twenty. The spirit which prompted him to try his hand at

47

everything and be defeated by nothing led him into unexpected channels. He occasionally wrote short stories, the theme generally being some incident in the hunting field. Though few of us saw these literary efforts, it was generally known that they existed, and he came in for a good deal of chaff, which did not in the least damp his ardour. He submitted them to various publications, and though none, as far as I know, ever appeared in print, he did not cease to hope that some day they would receive recognition.*

" Other instances of his minor activities might be quoted. He was in great demand at concerts, at which he told amusing stories with much gravity. In some Garrison churches it had become a custom for an officer to read the lessons. Bradford at once joined the ranks of those who were bold enough to undertake this duty, and as their numbers were few his willingness to do it was welcomed, and in addition he read very well.

" Performing at concerts and reading in church and such like things might have been regarded in many young subalterns as a desire to advertise and show off, which might have led to un-happy results. But Bradford went about his way very quietly, and with a peculiar dignity which made it unnecessary to employ repressive measures in order to save him from ' wind in the head.'

" So far I have only spoken of Bradford's social life in the Battalion, and in view of his won-derful career in war it would have been more fitting to have described first his military training. But when writing of a man distinguished in his career, it is not unusual to find efforts made to show that from the very beginning he displayed abnormal ability, and a thirst after perfection which obviously fore-

* Several of these stories did appear in magazines.

shadowed future greatness. Frequently the result is a picture of a professional prig.

" Bradford certainly did not burn the midnight oil poring over Hamley and Clausewitz, nor did he indulge in prophetic statements regarding the military art which have been fulfilled to the letter in this war.

" He went through his recruit's drill like any other subaltern, though no doubt with greater ease owing to a naturally quick mind and a well-made athletic body. When he had completed his recruit's drill and there was greater scope for his abilities, he displayed those high qualities most necessary in a good soldier—a high sense of honour, readiness to accept responsibility, an alert mind, rapidity in making decisions, and great energy combined with excellent physique.

" He was very keen when anything out of the common had to be done, when he had plenty of ideas and showed the courage of his convictions; but at times, like any other healthy subaltern, he found the necessary routine and petty duties of military work tiresome, and he had to be kept up to the mark in that respect.

" But to sum up, I do not think that anyone who knew him in peace was surprised that he succeeded in war, even to the height that he attained."

These, indeed, were happy days for Roland. Whether on parade, or in mess, playing games or hunting, discussing various questions with friends or writing stories that hard-hearted editors would not publish, he was living the life which he loved and had chosen, and he enjoyed every moment of it.

Many of those who knew him in these short years can testify to his boundless enthusiasm and wide interests.

Brigadier-General H. H. Morant, D.S.O., of the Durham Light Infantry, mentions two occasions on which his attention was attracted by Roland.

" Quite early I heard him discussing with and explaining to his brother ' subs.' the question of Kent coal. It seemed to me that I had never heard a subaltern of his age converse in such a capable and knowledgeable manner, and I never forgot his apparent business-like grasp of this subject.

" In 1914, playing cricket for the regiment, he was keeping wicket to an unusually fast bowler on a hard, bumpy wicket. He missed taking a ball which never touched his hands, but struck him direct on the temple and felled him instantly. The next moment he was up and ready to carry on with a bump as big as a turkey's egg already on his temple. I ordered him off, in spite of his vigorous protests, to have his head dressed. This gave me an indication of the innate and indomitable pluck for which he was famous afterwards."

During these short years before the War Roland was able to keep himself in perfect physical condition. He was not a teetotaller, but he drank very little, and as a smoker he was moderation itself. At various seasons of the year he played cricket, hockey and Rugby football, and when in the Midlands he hunted with the Atherstone and South Staffordshire hounds, and he also hunted in the Colchester district with the East Essex.

With his friends he was always ready to talk freely and to discuss any subject under the sun. But his chief pleasure lay in criticising tactics and military movements both destructively and constructively, and in discussing social and political problems. At this time, as far as it is possible to judge, his views seem to have been a mixture of sane Imperialism and moderate Socialism. He had, for instance, the keenest sympathy with the hard fate of the poorer wage-earners, and in no measured terms expressed his horror of the evils of an industrial system that permitted female labour to be sweated.

While quite a boy Roland had frequently tried to make inventions, but the lot of the inventor is always hard, and that of the young inventor especially so. Failure, however, did not in the least depress Roland. His attitude seemed to be that it was better to try and fail, than never to have tried at all. One of his inventions was a patent golf-club, but it never succeeded in winning popularity, nor was it calculated to make the game easier for those thousands of golfers who are waiting for a club that helps them to conquer their natural imperfections at the game. After joining the Army Roland turned his inventive powers to his professional work, and took out provisional patents for some of his ideas.

For a long time he experimented with an aluminium body shield which, because of its lightness, could be carried in the equipment of a soldier on the march and could be set up in front of him as a protection in the prone position. But on the rifle range he satisfied himself that aluminium had not the necessary bullet-resisting power, and with reluctance he abandoned this idea.

He afterwards thought out a system of protecting marching troops from the view of aeroplanes by means of fabric screens. On the air-raid alarm being given these screens were to be unfolded in lengths, and carried over the head of the column in a horizontal position by vertical stakes attached to the equipment of certain men in each section. This idea was actually tested by experts from the War Office, but it did not meet with their approval.

But the days when Roland had much spare time to give to inventions were numbered. July, 1914, came, and with it such a state of crisis that the thoughts of everyone in the British Isles, and indeed throughout the world, were turned to one subject. And that subject was War.

CHAPTER VII.

In July, 1914, the 2nd Battalion D.L.I. were in camp at Llanidloes, Wales, but when in the latter days of that month the danger of war grew nearer and nearer, they were hurriedly recalled to Lichfield.

Writing from Lichfield to his brother Tom on the 3rd of August Roland said : " We have not got the order to mobilise yet, but I don't see how we can keep out of this conflict. I expect you broke up your training. I enclose my cash book. All my scrip is at Messrs. Holt's. I have a stable and a large black forage shed behind the officers' mess here. All my kit is in this shed, and I will send you the key. In the event of my not returning it would be advisable for you personally to take away this kit (and sell the buildings). Unthank will take my mare out to the front, and in case of its loss you can claim £75. . . . I expect Georgie will be having an exciting time just now. Our men at the precautionary points would return on the second day of mobilisation, and would be relieved by the Special Reserve. To me this appears a unique opportunity of crushing Germany. I will write you before we move—if we do. Cheer-oh." And then he added a postscript, " I hear now that we are to mobilise."

It is a remarkably calm and sensible letter for a young and enthusiastic subaltern to write at a moment when he must have felt himself on the eve of great events, events for which he had been training himself strenuously in every way. Not a trace of excitement is to be found in these few lines to his brother, but they do show how thoughtful he had already learnt to be.

August was spent partly in Scotland and partly in Cambridge, and on September 9th, 1914, Roland embarked with his regiment for France, and landed at St. Nazaire on the following day. A fortnight later he was gazetted First-Lieutenant.

Of Roland at this period of his career Captain Welch, M.C., who knew him intimately, has written in eloquent words:

" Bradford for some time had foreseen the likelihood of war on a large scale. Now with dramatic suddenness it was here. He knew that for his nation it was a fight for existence, probably a long fight, and he was proud to take a part in it, glad that from the very beginning his place was in the arena and not among the spectators.

" He never had a doubt of the righteousness of the Allied cause, for he felt that Germany's arrogant pretensions were a threat to the future of civilisation. If ' Thrice-armed is he who knows his quarrel just,' Roland went well equipped into this life or death struggle of his country.

" The War offered infinite possibilities to the nation. What did it offer to him? What did he see, as he took rapid stock of his limitations and his potentialities? He was still a subaltern, a mere boy of 22, with no fighting experience; but he was sound in mind and body, and he had found that he could adapt himself to novel situations. This war, he felt, was to be the fiercest and bloodiest the world had ever known. There would be wide scope for the young, the self-disciplined, the imperturbable.

" It was to the possibility of rapid promotion that his mind naturally turned in the very early days of the War. Friends noted his confidence in himself, a confidence expressed with quiet certainty and without the least trace of undue self-assertion. He seemed to be assured that he had the latent ability to succeed in this the greatest of all games, as he had succeeded in his cricket and his hunting. Strong in body and a glutton for work, he could endure hardship and conquer circumstance. Master of himself, he could command men. Enthusiastic, he could kindle the ardour of others. Death had no terror for him, nor did he quail before the unknown future.

" Wordsworth's ideal soldier is he who, whether destined for fame or obscurity, *finds comfort in himself and in his cause.* This being so, no happier warrior than Bradford ever left England for the battle-fields of France."

The position in France in those early days of September is not likely to have been forgotten, but it must very briefly be mentioned.

The sweep of the German armies across North-Western France was held up by the battered but indomitable Allied forces. The German enveloping movement had failed, and on September 6th Marshal Joffre launched his counter-offensive. Slowly but steadily the enemy were driven back, and by the 12th they had been compelled to retire behind prepared defences on the Aisne and Suippes, upon which the immediate attack of the Allies led to no pronounced success. Within a week it had been realised that the position on the rivers was stalemate. So Joffre in turn attempted an enveloping movement by introducing new armies on the left of the British, but the success of this movement was prevented by the wariness of the Germans in lengthening their lines in parallel conformation.

This was the situation when the 2nd D.L.I. took their place in the British line on the Aisne. From the port of arrival the battalion proceeded by train to Coulommiers, and thence marched to St. Germain, where Roland's platoon did some outpost duty. Two or three days later they were at Soissons, and on September 20th they were engaged in the fighting on the river. Owing to the northward extension of the French line towards the sea, the British Army had been left between the two wings of the French Army. To remedy this unfortunate disposition a brilliantly executed movement took place in the first fortnight of October by which our army was transferred to the north, where it covered the Channel ports.

Captain Birt recalls an incident in this rearrangement of the line:

" Roland and I were in the closest contact for seven bad weeks, and I never saw him ' down ' a bit except once somewhere near Compiègne. We had been marching all night, and about 6 a.m. came upon the poor wretched refugees, old men, women of all ages and children on their way to Paris, with all their belongings on ' prams ' or in bundles. Roland was marching in the rear of the platoon, and suddenly he came up to me and said : ' Do you mind if I fall out for a few minutes?' On my liberating him he asked me for the spare bully beef and all the money I had (about 2 frs. 85), and he fell out, to rejoin about a quarter of an hour later, hot from his run and evidently cut up. After tramping at my horse's side for a few minutes he said : ' Did you see that last lot of refugees before I fell out? . . . There was a woman among them who reminded me of my mother.' "

In the mess Roland had often been chaffed as a woman-hater, harmless chaff enough, but in this case quite unreasonable. For his mother and sister he had a devotion that was supreme, and the miseries of French women and children, and the stories of brutality on the part of the enemy filled him with indignation. Whatever may be meant by the term woman-hater, Roland assuredly was not one.

By the middle of October the 2nd D.L.I. were near Armentières, and were having daily scraps with German cavalry outposts. In one of these, fought in pouring rain over water-logged fields, Roland, under an umbrella, which he had found in a deserted house, led his men to the attack.

Heavier fighting developed round Bois Grenier, where for three days our forces were continually engaged. On the third night of this fighting Roland's platoon was nearly surrounded, but by skilful leadership he rescued his tired men from a most awkward situation. Of this fighting one who took part in it has written : " We had another big do at Bois Grenier, and Lieut. R. B. Bradford proved at this period one of the finest officers I have ever had the pleasure of being with. We fought continually for two days and nights, but on the third night we were almost surrounded, and he gave me orders to watch the main road to Lille with three men ; and when I gave my report to him he brought us all out, and it was owing to his skill and valour that we got safely through."

It was in this sector that the battalion took up its position in the war of entrenchment that had developed.

In the early days of May, 1915, Roland was taken from his battalion and transferred as Lieutenant and Adjutant to the 7th Battalion, Durham Light Infantry. In a note to his mother, dated May 2nd, 1915, Roland mentions this :

> " I leave to-day to take over Adjutant of the 7th Battalion,
>> Durham Light Infantry,
>>> Northumbrian Division,
>>>> Expeditionary Force.
>>>>> (New address.)

I will probably not be able to write to you for a few days. Best love. Roland."

Very short as his letters from the front always and naturally were he wrote very frequently to his mother, and whenever it was possible he enclosed a little flower in his letter. It is really rather curious that even in chaff he had ever been accused of hating women.

Before Roland was transferred his qualities as a soldier had already begun to be officially recognised, as the following extracts supplied by the War Office will show :

(1) Lieutenant R. B. Bradford,
2nd Bn., Durham Light Infantry.
Awarded Military Cross in London Gazette dated 18th February, 1915.
" For services rendered in connection with operations in the field."

(2) Lieutenant R. B. Bradford,
2nd Bn., Durham Light Infantry.
Mentioned in Despatches, London Gazette, dated 17th February, 1915.
" For gallant and distinguished services in the field."

The Battalion to which Roland was transferred had only reached France about the middle of April, but it had already suffered severely in the second battle of Ypres, which had developed out of the action in which the enemy, in his attempt to smash through the salient to the coast, had used poisonous gas for the first time. In this battle the Battalion had lost heavily both in officers and men, Captain R. B. Bergne, the Adjutant, being one of the casualties. By a strange coincidence another R.B.B. was sent to fill his place.

Roland joined at Wateau, where the Battalion was resting after its terrible experiences in the line. His first parade was an official inspection by the Commander-in-Chief of the 151st Brigade, which contained the sadly-depleted 6th, 7th, 8th and 9th Battalions of the D.L.I.; Battalions which had already shown by clinging on to almost hopeless positions with splendid tenacity that they were worthy members of a regiment whose pride it is to be known as the " Faithful Durhams."

An eye-witness of this parade has described Roland as he was on that day.

" After our first action at Ypres, 1915 (in which our Adjutant was wounded, thus creating a vacancy), I first saw the late Brigadier, who had come (I presume) from the 2nd Batt. Durham L.I. as a Lieutenant, to fill the gap. The remnants of the 151st Brigade were drawn up for inspection by our Commander-in-Chief, then Sir John French.

" It was then that Lieut. Bradford, M.C. (as he was at that time), stood a striking silhouette to those who noticed him, alongside of our Colonel. A pleasanter smile no man could have seen than Lieut. Bradford's on that particular day, and he was among strangers of whom he could know nothing.

" Even in September, 1917, when I last shook

hands with him (prior to taking up his new command as Brigadier), he still had that old 1915 smile, but on a scarred face, caused by a wound that was not yet healed."

The routine work of a pioneer battalion, which the 7th D.L.I. became in November, 1915, was irksome, if not actually distasteful, to Roland, but he carried on with it until April, 1916, through a fine feeling of loyalty to Colonel Vaux. He longed to return to a line regiment, where there would naturally be a wider field in which to show his abilities. The time he served with the 7th D.L.I. gave him an opportunity to review the situation as it applied to himself, and during these quiet months he went strenuously to work to improve his knowledge of the French language, and he began to learn Spanish. He also took lessons in elocution by correspondence with a well-known London teacher, and, much to the amusement of those who saw him, he practised speaking and gesture before his mirror.

" Rather a peculiar manner he had at times, rather strange ways," one who served under him and admired him enormously has written. " For instance, he would pose in front of a looking-glass, and imitate (I should think) different actors, and he would also recite what he had read from a book, which he held behind his back."

Curious, indeed, must these little manœuvres have seemed to Roland's men, but as a matter of fact they were sensible enough, and all of them were practised as a means to a definite end. By this time he had become confident that he could be master of his own fate, and those of his friends who knew that his career was ruled by the maxim, " You can be whatever you resolve to be," took him without question at his own valuation.

Early in 1916 he was at home on leave, and discussed his future freely with Captain Welch.

" He was anxious," Captain Welch has said, " to become Brigade-Major of the Brigade, but he either felt or had been told that he looked too young. So he bought a large eye-glass which he wore for no other reason except to add the air of years and dignity that were lacking. He intended to be Brigade-Major, then a Battalion Commander, finally Brigade Commander. . . . And his friends at least were not surprised at his almost unparalleled rise to eminence in the months that followed."

During these months he also spent much time in writing, not, we are told, for amusement, but solely to train himself for the future when he would need words eloquent and convincing enough to influence and inspire the men he was to command.

Confident as Roland had become of himself he was not in the smallest degree conceited. Quite simply he was convinced of his abilities as a soldier, and he worked with all his might to perfect them. The War, from being merely a series of battles, had become to him a Cause. It was a fight to the end of Right against Might, and it seemed to him that any man who stood aside and failed to make the most of his gifts was shirking his duty. Personal ambition he had at the beginning of the War, and rightly had; Shakespeare speaks of ambition as the soldier's virtue; but all thoughts of self were soon obliterated by larger issues.

On his return from leave in February, 1916, Roland served for a time as Brigade-Major. The invariable practice at this time was that an officer, before being appointed to a Battalion, should serve as Second in Command, and in April, 1916, Roland left the 7th to join, in that capacity, the 9th Battalion of the D.L.I.

His departure was a source of genuine regret to all with whom he had come in contact. In a letter of congratulation his Colonel, Colonel Vaux, wrote: " Our year together has been, in my opinion, a very wonderful one. Never since you joined me have you and I had a single wrong word, and honestly I feel deeply all the things you have done for me."

These months with the 7th Battalion had given Roland a chance to familiarise himself with all the intricate detail of battalion organisation, and also they had given him a breathing space which he used mainly in preparing himself for the future which he felt was in store for him.

CHAPTER VIII.

In the beginning of May, 1916, Roland joined the 9th Battalion of the Durham Light Infantry at Mount Cockerill. The 9th had just been through a most strenuous time in the southern part of the Ypres Salient, their last period of trench duty having lasted over a month; and in May they were resting and training in a delightfully peaceful spot not far behind the line.

Of this place Roland wrote to his brother, Captain Bradford: " We are resting now—near the place where you were—in hospital just before you left." And then, with the true Bradford touch, he added, " I am temporary Major—so mind that you click your heels smartly when you next see me !"

A Territorial Battalion, the 9th, like the 7th, went out to France in April, 1915, with the Northumbrian (50th) Division, and within a week of landing were rushed up into the Ypres Salient to repel the German attacks. Since then they had fought, trained and rested until they had become a seasoned battalion with a well-established reputation.

As Second in Command, and then as Commanding Officer, Roland remained with this battalion until November, 1917, a period of eighteen months. During this time he enhanced its reputation and helped to create in it a fighting spirit that made it famous throughout France.

" We are all right," an officer in another battalion · was heard to say, " the 9th are on our right."

On May 28th, their period of rest having ended, the 9th took over part of the Kemmel Sector, familiar ground to them, and there they carried on ordinary trench routine until August 8th, when the 50th Division moved south to take part in the operations on the Somme. Roland, Lieutenant-Colonel from August 4th, was by this time in command of the 9th, and during the three weeks of strenuous training that followed at Baizieux he began to mould the battalion in his own fashion.

The great Somme battle was in its tenth week, and the attack on the strongly fortified Courcelette-Morval position was just beginning. The new weapon of war, the Tank, was being used for the first time as a fighting unit.

On September 14th the 9th moved forward to the old German lines near Mametz Wood, and on the following day were in the thick of the battle. As part of the 151st Brigade the 9th were at first in reserve, but early in the attack orders were received that they were to move up in support of part of the 149th Brigade.

In the ensuing action Roland was hit by a piece of shell, which caused a nasty flesh wound. " But," Major Crouch, his second in command, has written, " the tenacious spirit of the C.O., which would not be denied the honour of leading his battalion into action, kept him at duty. What he suffered physically by this noble act he alone knew, but I do know that two months later it was still necessary for the M.O. to dress his wound."

It may not be inappropriate here to mention that Roland was " officially " wounded on three occasions. " 15th September, 1916, 16th January, 1917, and 5th November, 1917. On each occasion Brigadier-General Bradford remained at duty."

In reference to this attack the Commanding Officer of another battalion writes : " At a meeting of the C.O.'s at 8.30 p.m. on that day Bradford was present and said very little. A plan of attack was being drawn up by the Brigadier, and the hour he at first fixed was, I think, 10. At this point Bradford spoke and said he thought it was too early. It was put off until, I think, 10.30. . . . Bradford during this attack was up in the front line of his battalion, and back in Clarke's trench, and continually moving about with the most surprising vigour. He went forward with one attack and carried a wounded man back under heavy fire to the assembly trench."

To appreciate deservedly the grit and determination that Roland showed during this attack, it is necessary to realise that during the whole time when the 9th were working their way forward they were being subjected to a most intense machine gun fire from the enemy's trenches, and from the high ground near High Wood. So devastating was this fire that they were unable to reach their objective, though they consolidated a position in No Man's Land and grimly clung to it until they were relieved on the night of September 22nd.

Thus the first phase of the Somme fighting ended as far as it concerned the 9th D.L.I. It was their first severe test under their new Colonel, and from that time onward it is the simple truth that their faith in him was only equalled by his faith in them.

A few days, not of rest but of less strenuous work, followed in the comparative security of the German dug-outs. Then, on September 28th, they were ordered into the " Seven Elms " area to take part in the attack upon Eaucort L'Abbaye.

On October 1st, with the rest of the 50th Division, they moved forward, at first in support.

Early in the day difficulties began to happen on the right, owing to the 47th and 50th Divisions losing touch. A battalion in the leading line suffered heavily, its Commander was wounded, and this flank of the Division became dangerously exposed.

It was at this critical time that Roland showed his real genius for war. Before the enemy could take advantage of the break he had seen the danger, and the remedy immediately occurred to his quick, tactical mind.

With the consent of the wounded Commander, Roland agreed to take over the command of the exposed battalion, the 6th D.L.I., in addition to his own. He at once proceeded to the foremost lines, and " by his fearless energy under fire of all descriptions and his skilful leadership of the two battalions, regardless of all danger, he succeeded in rallying the attack, captured and held the objective, and so secured the flank."

The following account, which Major G. E. Wilkinson, commanding the 6th Battalion D.L.I., has contributed, will amply explain the nature and extent of Roland's achievement at this critical time :

" On the 27th September, 1916, I took over command of the 6th D.L.I., who were then in reserve trenches behind High Wood, and on that night I had to move the battalion up to closer reserve to support an attack which the 1st Division were carrying out.

" On the 28th September I was ordered to relieve the 4th Yorkshires, commanded by Colonel Deacon, and in the early morning of the 30th September at 5 a.m. I went up to find out the whereabouts of Colonel Bradford and his battalion, who, I understood, were on my left. His Headquarters were at the Seven Elms, and I found him in the front line directing the digging of trenches by his battalion.

" I inquired whether he knew the strength of the German front line, which was the Flers line running through Eaucort L'Abbaye, and he replied that if I would wait for a little time he was just going out with a party of bombers to try and find out its strength. The morning was very foggy, and when he came back after a noisy quarter of an hour, he said that in his opinion they were holding the line pretty strongly, and that he had been unable to effect an entry into the trenches in spite of the fog.

" Bradford afterwards showed me round what trenches he had dug and pointed out to me what he thought ought to be his front line trench, but owing to the fog his men had dug the trench at right angles instead of parallel to the Boche. I informed him that this would suit me very well for a communication trench, as I anticipated that I should shortly be coming up to relieve him.

" I got back to my Headquarters about 9 a.m., and General Cameron, who was commanding the 151st Brigade, arrived soon afterwards with his Brigade-Major, and told me that the 6th D.L.I. would have to attack on the afternoon of the 1st October at 3 o'clock, and that he wished me to take steps to relieve Bradford forthwith, as he was getting the 9th D.L.I. into reserve.

" I told him that I had just been up to see Bradford, and he accordingly ordered me to proceed with the relief, which I did. Owing to the fact that I had to go back to my Brigade Headquarters some three or four miles back, for a conference, I did not formally complete the relief of the 9th D.L.I. until well after dark. I, however, saw Bradford at his Headquarters at Seven Elms, and we decided that it would be necessary for me to establish my Headquarters nearer the Boche so as to be in touch with my men for the attack, and he accordingly decided to remain at Seven Elms. We discussed the digging of trenches, and I spent the whole night, until dawn, with my men digging two lines of assembly trenches for the attack.

" On the morning of the 1st October, owing to the fact that our trenches were only three feet deep, we suffered considerable casualties through sniping and shell fire. About three-quarters of an hour before the time of the attack I was going round to see that everything was in order, as, owing to the transport being three or four miles behind I had had great difficulty in getting up ammunition and rations, and while I was discussing details with a sergeant the man next to me was shot through the neck.

" As the men were huddled together, I got out of the trench to pass the wounded man, and while I was looking at the lie of the land from the top of the trench, the same sniper who had hit the man next to me hit me and smashed my arm, thus making it necessary for me to go back before the attack.

" On my way back I went in and saw Colonel Bradford and his Adjutant at his Headquarters at Seven Elms and told him of the situation, and I suggested to him that he should go up and take command of the 6th D.L.I. in addition to the 9th. I told him that it was imperative to have a senior officer up to control matters, as I had no one in my battalion except lieutenants and second-lieutenants.

" I then proceeded on my way back and met the Brigadier and his Brigade-Major, two miles behind, coming up to their Battle Headquarters, and I told them what I had arranged with Colonel Bradford, and he immediately approved of my action.

" I heard afterwards from the Adjutant of the 6th D.L.I. about the attack, and apparently what happened was that the two left companies of the 6th D.L.I. got through to their objective, but the second two companies on the right were practically cut to bits.

" Bradford rallied the remains of these companies and, with the assistance of his own men, who were moving up in support when I went down wounded, organised a bombing attack down the trench to the right, and established touch with the 47th Division who were on the right, but at the time of the attack had not reached their battle position. Captain Ebsworth (Adjutant of the 6th D.L.I.) spoke in glowing terms of Col. Bradford's organising ability, which only confirmed my own opinion of what a very fine soldier he was.

" Col. Bradford also wrote to me when in hospital later on and told me what had happened, and was very modest about his own efforts in the matter."

As regards this tremendous fighting on October 1st, 1916, Major Veitch, M.C., has written some notes that throw a strong light on Roland himself and on what his presence meant to others :

" Lt.-Col. Bradford was first recommended for the D.S.O. by Br.-Gen. Cameron, but as fuller details of his action became known this recommendation was withdrawn, and he was recommended for the V.C. instead. On 1st October immediately after the successful attack I went to his Headquarters at ' Seven Elms,' about half a mile in front of High Wood. Colonel Bradford had only a very short time before returned from leading the attack, and I was astonished to find him looking as though he had ' just stepped out of his tailor's.' Looking at him, it was difficult to realise that less than an hour before he had been in the thick of the fighting. It was all in keeping with his strong belief in the moral effect of his presence and appearance on those he came into contact with. He certainly inspired confidence in everyone who saw him at that time when things were decidedly uncomfortable, and very uncertain. It was a little thing, but I came away feeling that everything was all right. In other words, ' It did all of us good to see him.' "

In a supplement to the *London Gazette,* issued on Saturday, November 25th, 1916, the award of the Victoria Cross was announced in the following terms :—

"Lieut.-Col. ROLAND BOYS BRADFORD, D.L.I.

"Lieut. (temporary Lieut.-Col.) Roland Boys Bradford, M.C., Durham Light Infantry, for most conspicuous bravery and good leadership in attack, whereby he saved the situation on the right flank of his brigade and of the division. Lt.-Col. Bradford's battalion was in support. A leading battalion having suffered very severe casualties, and the commander being wounded, its flank became dangerously exposed at close quarters to the enemy. Raked by machine gun fire, the situation of the battalion became critical. At the request of the wounded commander Lt.-Col. Bradford asked permission to command the exposed battalion in addition to his own. Permission granted, he at once proceeded to the foremost lines. By his fearless conduct under fire of all description and his skilful leadership of the two battalions, regardless of all danger, he succeeded in rallying the attack, captured and defended the objective and so secured the flank."

Nothing in Roland's brilliant career was more indicative of his genius for war than this incident, which won for him the highest reward that any nation offers for valour. It is not the smallest exaggeration to say that, for its successful accomplishment, the highest qualities of a great leader in the field were required.

Writing after Roland had been killed Brigadier-General Morant said: "When Bradford was awarded the V.C. I had an officer who served with him in 1914 as a sergeant on the Aisne. When this officer saw the announcement he could not have been more delighted if the V.C. had been awarded to himself."

When the announcement of the award was made known, the 9th were at Mellincourt on the Somme, and it is little to be wondered at that the delight of both officers and men was irrepressible. In spite of Roland's efforts to get away he was chaired, and all appeals to be put down were drowned in deafening cries of "Speech, speech."

Ultimately he did say a few words, in which he would not admit that he had earned the reward himself, but declared that it was a tribute to the good work accomplished by the whole battalion.

On the 6th of October, after three weeks hard and successful fighting, Roland had taken his sadly-depleted and weary, but also confident, men back to Hennicourt Wood for rest, re-organisation and training. They ploughed their way back, pulling Lewis gun barrows through fields and over roads so sodden that every step was an effort, but in spite of this desperate toil not one man discarded the Boche helmets, caps and souvenirs so dear to the heart of the British soldier.

The 9th stayed in rest-quarters for nearly a month, and during that period Roland looked after the welfare of his men with the same untiring zeal and devotion that he had shown in the line.

Within two days the men had visited the Divisional baths, and had been supplied with new underclothing and uniforms. An inter-platoon football competition was soon in full swing, and the organisation of a battalion band was under consideration.

During the late autumn of 1916 Roland wrote several letters to Lord Northbourne, the Honorary Colonel of the 9th, which show, if proof is needed, how proud of and zealous for his men he was.

In the first letter he wrote :—

" Dear Lord Northbourne,

" I write to let you know the doings of the Battalion during the Somme offensive.

" We went into the battle first on the 15th September, when we assisted in taking the enemy trenches between High Wood and Martinpuich. After a fortnight's hard fighting our Division captured the Flers front and support lines.

" The men of this Battalion fought conspicuously well and with great gallantry. In all we had 70 officers and men killed and 400 wounded. . . . The men are all happy and fit and eager again to meet the accursed Germans.

" I send you a reproduction of a drawing of the Cross I had erected N.W. of High Wood in memory of the officers and men of the 9th D.L.I. who fell in the Somme offensive. I have organised a Band, which is a great boon to all ranks. I know you will have a great many claims on you just now, but I venture to ask you for one or two things. First of all I enclose a list of music which perhaps you could see your way to obtaining and sending to us. Do you think that during the winter you could send out a weekly parcel for the men of, say, polonies, cakes, kippers, condensed milk, and a few socks?

" In the cold weather the great thing is to be able to feed the inner man.

" Candles, too, are very acceptable.

" Please forgive me for worrying you in this matter, but I feel you will not mind.

" Everything is going well out here—we have the absolute ascendency of the enemy.

" Best wishes,

"Yours sincerely,
" Roland Bradford,
" Lt.-Col., Cmdg. 9th D.L.I."

Although without musical talent himself Roland loved music, and also knew how valuable and stimulating it was to those who were fighting their country's battles. In addition to the band he also superintended the formation of " The Green Diamonds," a troupe of entertainers who gave many excellent concerts under varied, and often adverse conditions. Very readily did the troupe acknowledge that their success was largely due to their C.O.'s support and persistent interest in them.

Roland also introduced a custom that will never be forgotten by any man who served in the 9th. Every night, whether in rest billets or in the trenches, his men sang some verses of " Abide with me." Upon occasions the hymn would be started in one shell hole, and taken up by the next post, until the whole line joined in.

Frequently the enemy must have heard it and wondered; its accompaniment was often played by the artillery of friends and foes alike. That this custom had a deep effect on the minds of all ranks cannot be denied; abundant evidence exists to prove it.

On the 1st November, the 50th Division were again in the line, and four days later made a magnificent and determined attack on the formidable Butte de Warlencourt, in which the 9th played a most important part.

CHAPTER IX.

Of this fighting in the early days of November, 1916, Roland wrote so clear and valuable an account that it is more than worthy of record.

" The Attack made by the 50th Division
on the Butte de Warlencourt
and
The Gird Line
on November 5th, 1916.

" In the first week of November, 1916, there had been heavy rain in the Somme area and the surface of the ground was thick with mud.

" It was impossible to use any of the communication trenches, and movement across the open, even right behind our lines where you were unmolested by enemy fire, was attended with great difficulty and was very exhausting.

" The front line held by the 50th Division in the first week in November was Maxwell Trench, which lay immediately east of the Albert-Bapaume road and ran first behind the Southern Crest of the small ridge on which the Butte-de-Warlencourt was situated. This trench opposite the Butte was separated by a distance of 250 yards, and throughout its length was an average distance of 300 yards from the German front line.

" On November 5th, the 151st Infantry Brigade was to attack in conjunction with the Australians on the right. The 46th Division on the left was not going to attack, but was to co-operate with fire. The objectives of the Brigade were the capture of the Butte, the Quarry and the Gird front line on the left, and to capture and consolidate the Gird front line and support lines on the right.

" Three Battalions of the 151st Infantry Brigade were to assault, each Battalion being on a frontage of three Companies with one Company in reserve, which was to remain in Maxwell Trench. The 9th D.L.I. was on the left, the 6th D.L.I. in the centre, and the 8th D.L.I. on the right.

" The 5th Border Regiment was in Brigade Reserve and was in readiness in the trenches north of Eaucort L'Abbaye. The 6th Battalion N.F. was attached to the Brigade as a further reserve and was situated in the Flers Support Line just west of Eaucort L'Abbaye.

" At 9 a.m. the assaulting Infantry moved forward. These troops were in four lines with a distance of 15 yards between each.

" The 6th D.L.I. and the 8th D.L.I. had only gone forward about 50 yards when they came under very heavy machine gun fire which caused many casualties and prevented them from reaching their objectives, although many heroic efforts to get forward were made. The Australians on the right were met by intense machine gun fire, and they were also unable to make any progress.

" On the left the 9th D.L.I. met with less opposition, and succeeded in gaining all its objectives without suffering heavy casualties. The German barrages came down at about four minutes after nine o'clock. There were three barrages, one was a few yards in advance of Maxwell Trench, another was on Hexham Road where Battalion Headquarters was situated in a dugout at the entrance to Snag Trench, and the third was between Hexham Road and the Flers line. All were particularly intense.

" At 10 a.m. the 9th D.L.I. was disposed as follows : —

" Four posts were established in the Gird Front Line, the left one being in the Albert-Bapaume Road. There were four Posts in the space between the Butte and the Gird Front Line. The front edge of the Quarry was strongly held and two Company Headquarters were situated in the Quarry in telephonic communication with Battalion Headquarters. Each of the assaulting Platoons had a reserve Platoon on Butte Alley, the trench running immediately South of the Butte. Two machine guns were sited in Butte Alley and a 2in. Stokes Mortar in the Quarry. Two Battalion Observers were on the Butte. The Reserve Company of the Battalion was in Maxwell Trench. Eight Bavarian prisoners had been sent back to the Battalion Headquarters, Some other prisoners who were on their way back had, together with their escort, been annihilated by the German Artillery fire.

" The Germans were still holding a dugout on the North East side of the Butte. The Parties who should have ' mopped up ' the Butte dugouts had either gone forward without completing their work, carried away in the enthusiasm of the assault, or had been shot by German snipers while at their work. The ground had been so pulverised by our bombardments and was so muddy that it was impossible to do much in the way of consolidation. But the men were ready with their rifles.

" The Germans had by this time realised the scope of our attack, and many of their Batteries concentrated their fire on our new positions. Snipers from Warlencourt-Eaucort were subjecting our men to a deadly fire, and it was almost impossible for them to move.

" The Germans in the dugout on the North-East edge of the Butte had brought a machine gun into position, and were worrying us from behind. Many gallant attempts were made throughout the day to capture this dugout, but without success. All our parties who tried to rush it were destroyed by the German machine gun fire from the direction of Hook Sap, and by the fire of the large number of snipers in Warlencourt. However, our party did succeed in throwing some Mill's grenades into the dugout, and this made the Boches more cautious.

" The first German counter-attack was made about 12 noon. It was a half-hearted one and was easily stopped. During the afternoon the enemy launched several bombing attacks, but these were also repulsed.

" About 6 p.m. the Germans made a determined counter-attack which was preceded by a terrific bombardment, and they were able to get to close quarters. A tough struggle ensued. But our men, who had now been reinforced by the Reserve Company, showed the traditional superiority of the British in hand-to-hand fighting, and succeeded in driving out the enemy.

" The 9th D.L.I. was getting weak, but it was hoped that the Boche had now made his last counter-attack for that day. It had happened that the Bavarian Division, which was holding the line when we attacked, was to have been relieved on the night of the 5th/6th November by the Prussian Guards Division.

" At about 11 p.m. Battalions of the Prussians

delivered a fresh counter-attack. They came in great force from our front, and they also worked round from both flanks. Our men were overwhelmed. Many died fighting. Others were compelled to surrender. It was only a handful of men who found their way back to the Maxwell Trench, and they were completely exhausted by their great efforts and by the strain of fighting.

" There were many reasons why the 9th D.L.I. was unable to hold its ground. The failure of the troops on the right to reach their objective, and the fact that the Division on our left was not attacking, caused both flanks of the Battalion to be in the air. The positions to be held were very much exposed, and the Germans could see all our movements and control their fire accordingly. It was a local attack, and the enemy was able to concentrate his guns on to a small portion of our line. The ground was a sea of mud, and it was almost impossible to consolidate our posts. The terribly intense German barrages and the difficult nature of the ground prevented reinforcements from being sent up to help the 9th D.L.I.

" Four hundred yards north of the Butte the enemy had a steep bank, behind which they were able to assemble without being molested. In the hope of being able to exploit success we had arranged for our barrage to be placed just beyond this bank. The terrain was very favourable to a German counter-attack. In addition to the splendid observation points in their possession the ground provided great facilities for the forming up of troops under cover.

" At first sight it might appear as if the conditions were somewhat reciprocal, for we had the Maxwell Trench ridge, which gave us some cover. But it was not really so. The ground between the

Flers Line and Hexham Road before getting under cover of the Maxwell Trench ridge is very exposed, and all the ground concealed by the ridge was intensely shelled by the enemy throughout the day and night.

" It is wonderful, when one considers the difficulties under which our men were working, and the fearful fire to which they were exposed, that they held on as long as they did. And it makes one proud to be an Englishman.

" On looking back at the attack of the 15th of November, it seems that the results which would have been gained in the event of success were of doubtful value, and would hardly have been worth the losses which we were bound to suffer. It would have been awkward for us to hold the objective, which would have been badly sited for our defence.

" The possession of the Butte by the Germans was not an asset to them. From our existing trenches we were able to prevent them from using it as an observation point.

" The Butte itself would have been of little use to us for purposes of observation.

" But the Butte-de-Warlencourt had become an obsession. Everybody wanted it. It loomed large in the minds of the soldiers in the forward area and they attributed many of their misfortunes to it. The newspaper correspondents talked about that ' Miniature Gibraltar.' So it had to be taken.

" It seems that the attack was one of those tempting, and unfortunately at one period frequent, local operations which are so costly, and which are rarely worth while.

" But perhaps this is only the narrow view of the Regimental Officer."

On November 6th, what was left of the Battalion—ninety-four officers and men in all, including Headquarters—was withdrawn from the line into camp near Mametz Wood. They had gallantly captured and held for eighteen hours a position which had often been previously attacked but had never been held. But at a terrible loss of life.

Some months later Roland had the honour of conducting H.R.H. the Duke of Connaught round the Butte and of explaining these November operations to him.

After the fighting of Warlencourt the remnants of the 9th Durham L.I. had a short period of road-mending, and then they moved back to rest and re-organise in the vicinity of Warley.

Strong reinforcements arrived from home and Roland, with tireless energy, set to work at once to imbue them with the same spirit and dash that had made their predecessors in the battalion so famous. His methods of training were always strenuous and often original, demanding much from both officers and men; but at the same time the equally important question of the amusement and comfort of his soldiers received his continuous personal attention, and he could sympathise with their disappointment as keenly as he could rejoice at their bravery. After the attack on the Butte de Warlencourt the Rev. Cyril Lomax, who served as Chaplain with Roland, has mentioned an incident which shows how very real this sympathy was.

" I conceived," Mr. Lomax has written, " the greatest affection and admiration for Roland while I was serving with him. He was hardly ever absent from Church Parade, and was always most willing to back up the efforts of the Chaplain. I remember him asking me on Nov. 12th, 1916, to speak to the men about the losses they had sustained in an attack which was quite successful in taking the Butte, though afterwards, owing to want of support, the 9th were forced to retire. He told me how much the men felt it, and he seemed to feel it even more keenly for their sakes. . . . I should imagine that he carried less personal kit than many of his subalterns; his personal wants were modest. Quiet, always fresh and unworried, he bore the strain of mud and shell in a marvellous way.

" I do not think his success had in the slightest degree turned his head, or made it swell.

" He must have exerted a great influence for good in his mess, as one never heard an objectionable story there.

" His energy was so great that no detail was too small for his consideration if it helped the men. I remember going to see him once in his tent and finding him busy with a model bomb which he had ordered from England. A section was cut out of the bomb to show the working inside, so that dense recruits might be helped to understand the working.

" He was always about among his men. This and his coolness were the main causes of his success. When I went up to the line to bury he always attended. And I recollect that one day up in the support trenches near Flers, opposite the Butte de Warlencourt, he came out to the burial of one of his men, and then asked me if I would like to go with him to hunt for some Boche dugouts along a ridge. Two officers whom he had sent to find them had failed to do so (the situation was not over-healthy), and so he proposed to go himself.

" He was extraordinarily helpful under shell-fire, and he humbugged me for not ducking quick enough when they came along. We found the dug-outs, and then proceeded to bury some Australians who were lying near. Of course this was under enemy observation.

" It was only natural that the men thought all the world of him. I remember the tremendous ovation he received from the battalion when news of his V.C. came through.

" Yet he was strict. But his strictness and keenness were all to help the men to be proud of their battalion and sure of themselves. In this he succeeded so thoroughly that some people said (so many were the decorations won by the 9th) that any N.C.O. of the 9th appearing on parade without a medal ribbon was put under arrest for being improperly dressed!"

The winter of 1916-17 was extremely severe, and in consequence exceptionally trying for all troops who were serving in France. But until the end of 1916 the 9th were engaged in reorganising and resting after its terrible ordeals. During these weeks Roland, as his letters to Lord Northbourne show, never ceased to think of the comfort of his men.

In a letter written in the middle of November he thanks Lord Northbourne for so promptly sending the music, and says that the Band were already busy practising some of the pieces.

" The men," he adds, " are wonderful. In spite of our losses they are happy and well, and thoroughly keen to have another go at the Boche."

A month later he wrote again : " I have just bought five pigs for the men's Christmas dinner. We ought not to be extravagant just now, but an occasional ' bust ' is the men's due. . . . At our last concert a vote of thanks was passed to you for the music you so kindly sent us. I have another little favour to ask you. We are now holding a Football Tournament, and I want to present gold medals to the winning team, and silver ones to the runners-up. That would be eleven gold medals and eleven silver ones. Do you think you could send out these? If you can I would like to have them by Dec. 31st. The design I would like on the medals would be the D.L.I. Badge on the Obverse, and the following on the Reverse:

" ' 9th D.L.I. Football Tournament, December, 1916.' But I leave the design entirely to you, and daresay some of the shops have suitable ready-made designs. You would be very proud of my boys—and *your* boys—if you could see them. I suppose it would be too much to ask a busy man like you to come over and inspect us."

Three days later Roland was, with many apologies, writing again to Lord Northbourne, but he had forgotten something, and in his haste to rectify the omission shows very clearly how thoroughly he understood the feelings of his men.

After asking for more music and promising not to worry again for a long time, he says : " If you have not already sent the medals I wonder if you could send twelve gold and silver ones instead of eleven. Two of my N.C.O.'s have been doing fine work in organising and arranging the football, and I would like to give them one each. The men love a medal, and especially as it comes from you. I send you my best wishes for the New Year. I shall be sending you the Battalion New Year card in a day or two."

But before the medals could arrive from England the 9th's period of rest was over, and on December 28th they returned to carry out ordinary trench duty.

During the first six weeks of the New Year a severe frost made living in the open a stern test of stamina, but the absence of mud was a compensation, the extent of which can hardly be realised by those who did not experience the awful conditions that had previously prevailed.

But the end of the frost brought with it more intensified discomfort than any that had yet been endured. During the thaw trenches silted in and were obliterated, and those who tried to move about in them literally stuck in the mud and either had to wait for assistance or proceed bare-foot, leaving thigh boots behind them.

In February the 9th were resting for a short time, and Roland wrote once more to Lord Northbourne thanking him for the medals.

Dear Lord Northbourne,

The medals arrived yesterday and I presented them to the men to-day. They were beautiful medals, and I have never seen a prettier or more neatly worked design. The men were delighted with them. It was extremely kind of you to take so much trouble in the matter.

The men are all happy and well.

We are having severe frost out here, which I see in the papers is what you are having at home. We are all wondering what America will do this time.

I hope you are keeping well.

We are resting at present, and have very comfortable billets.

We are going to play the 3rd Coldstream Guards at football to-morrow.

With best wishes,

Yours very sincerely,

3.2.17.   ROLAND BRADFORD.

Soon after this letter was written the 9th were back again in the trenches, struggling not only against the enemy but also against the appalling mud which the thaw had brought in its wake.

———

CHAPTER X.

After Roland had been awarded the V.C. in November, 1916, he came home on ten days' leave, and while he was in London an incident occurred which must have been as ironical as any of a similar kind that happened during the War.

He was standing one day in Hyde Park and listening to a speaker who was talking wildly about the Irish problem and the War. Eventually Roland ventured to ask one or two searching questions, which annoyed the speaker so much that instead of replying to them he asked why such a strong healthy man was not fighting instead of lounging about in Hyde Park. And the end of this incident was that Roland, who characteristically refused to reveal his identity, was loudly booed by a hostile crowd. Irony could scarcely go further.

During this leave Roland also visited Darlington, and the Mayor asked if he might arrange a public welcome. To this invitation Roland replied that if anything of the sort were done he should get straight into a train and return to London. This answer, curt as it seems, was not due to the smallest intention of being discourteous, but solely to the fact that the longer the War lasted the less, in Roland's opinion, did any individual deserve any public fêting. Whatever personal ambition he had ever had was entirely obliterated by his love for and pride in his men. The honour that had been conferred on him was an honour to his battalion even more than to himself. He had said this, and quite honestly he meant it. Without any doubt he would have agreed unhesitatingly with the letter which Francis Grenfell, on hearing that he had won the V.C., wrote to his uncle.

" I have been through so much since June, that what would and should have made me yell with joy nearly causes tears. It gave me no great feeling of having achieved anything. I feel that I know so many who have done and are doing so much more than I have been able to do for England. I also feel very strongly that any honour belongs to my regiment and not to me. They have paid the toll and will go on paying until the road is clear."

During the last months of his short life Roland was, as ever, thoughtful of his mother, sister, and brothers, but apart from this his mind was set solely on two considerations. The first was that his men should be as perfectly trained and as happy as possible, the second that as much time as he could spare should be given to thinking out plans and schemes to defeat the enemy. " The secret of success," Lord Beaconsfield said, " is constancy to purpose," and undoubtedly Roland proved the truth of these words.

" I was in close touch with him," one of his men has written, " from December, 1916, to April, 1917, he being then C.O. of the 9th Battalion of the Durham Light Infantry. For although I was only a private I saw a lot of him in connection with the formation of a ' Battalion Concert Party,' which he proudly labelled ' The Green Diamonds.'

" In his never tiring efforts to bring some sunshine into the precarious lives of the men under his charge, he quickly discovered on my joining his battalion that my civilian occupation was that of an actor, and he promptly sent for me. And he did not rest until the first performance of ' The Green Diamonds ' at Marycourt was *un fait accompli.*"

From another letter it can be understood that when once " The Green Diamonds " had started they were not to be stopped from performing by inconveniences great or small. " I remember," Mr. Lomax has said, " that on April 22nd, 1917, at Romville, outside Arras, a fine Pierrot troupe in costume from the 9th, called ' The Green Diamonds,' from the distinguishing badge on their tunic sleeves, gave a show, up against a piece of ruined wall. Shells dropped near, and the audience sat in shell holes."

It has already been said that some of Roland's ideas were original, and possibly none was more so than his order that his men should during the summer months take Sun Baths.

Watching closely over the health of the men he had been impressed by the amount of skin disease that existed among them. So he consulted the Regimental Medical Officer, and having been assured that Sun Bathing would be beneficial for this disease he issued an order that the men, whether in the line or resting, should sit naked in the sun for an hour each day.

At first the modesty of the men prevented them from approving of his command, but Roland never expected any man to do a thing that he was not prepared to do himself, and after he had given them a lead the difficulty very soon was not to get them to take off their clothes but to see that they put them on again at the end of the hour. And we are told that this daily Sun Bath had a wonderfully good effect on the condition of the men.

To prevent the casualties and fatigue that were invariably associated with ration parties Roland developed the plan of taking rations up to the front line on mules. With the humour natural to the British soldier this cavalcade was promptly christened " Bradford's Cavalry " by the men of other battalions.

So eager, indeed, was he to devise and find out any plan for beating the enemy that he applied to go to a French Division to take part in an attack with them. He wanted, he said, to see how the French fought. Nothing came of this application, but in no wise discouraged, Roland continued to study daily, and he encouraged his officers to follow his example.

A letter from Mr. H. C. B. Plummer, who was Roland's Intelligence Officer, from March, 1917—November, 1917, is of great interest, for it comes from one who was in the closest touch with him during that period.

" Conscientiousness," Mr. Plummer says, " was the outstanding feature of his character, and from this sprang the other virtues, of which he had so many. His personal energy and strict attention to detail were the cause, more than anything else, of his success in all military undertakings, while his wide experience gave him an extraordinary power of grasping any situation.

" His love of music led him to form a band, which he regarded as a necessity for a battalion. . . .

" In religious matters he showed himself to be a sincere Christian, and at the close of each day he brought his battalion together to sing his favourite hymn, ' Abide with me.' . . .

" In the third battle of Ypres this hymn was played by our band at Marsouin Farm on Pilken Ridge. There we were too close to the enemy to be able to assemble the men, and so they sang it grouped in twos or threes in their bivouacs.

" He often spoke to his battalion before or after an engagement, and on one occasion I remember him telling them not to be ashamed to pray.

" He aimed at acquiring personal knowledge of all his officers and men, and, with this object in view, he held individual conversations with all under his command, whether senior officer or private soldier. He had an extraordinary memory and knew almost every man by name, despite the frequent changes that took place."

Then, after mentioning the Sun Baths, and Roland's keenness on the men's games and sports, Mr. Plummer continues :

" In these as in all other respects, the men saw in him their true friend, and, as such, they supported him to their utmost throughout.

" While realising the privileges due to officers, he believed that they ought to share certain discomforts with the men, notably the carrying of a pack on the march. If the men were wearing steel helmets he invariably wore his, and once when he was returning to the battalion, he borrowed a runner's steel helmet, so that he might take the salute ' properly dressed,' as he called it. To junior officers particularly he was always willing to give advice and help, and many, like myself, have every reason to be grateful to him.

" He was always very particular about the personal appearance of his men, and dealt very severely with those he saw not wearing a cap badge or with a button undone. As he rode on parade on his grey mare it became instinctive to everyone to make a rapid survey of one's buttons."

Mr. Plummer then goes on to say how great was the importance Roland attached to training.

" No C.O. attached more importance to training than he did. When the battalion was out of the line he arranged strenuous courses to fit it for any eventuality that might occur in the line. Comprehensive as they were they naturally involved long hours.

" At Warluzel, in May, 1917, we paraded at 7 a.m., ostensibly to avoid the heat of the day, but in reality to have longer hours at our disposal. During the first few mornings the first hour was so cold that physical exercises or games were essential to keep the men warm. You may imagine that humorous remarks about ' the heat of the day ' were to be heard on all sides. . . .

" Field firing practices were perhaps the favourite of our C.O.'s schemes, and are illustrative of his desire to make training as realistic as possible."

After these strenuous mornings Roland would not infrequently spend the afternoon in giving a lecture to his officers and senior N.C.O.'s, and sometimes he would set a subject on which the officers were to write an essay. And in the evenings he almost invariably watched or took part in the men's games.

" Energetic," Mr. Plummer continues, " out of the line he was far more so in the line. His unfailing daily visit under all conditions and talks with the men in the trenches cemented the friendship which always existed between them.

" It was in the trenches, too, that one saw his true worth. Supremely brave, but never reckless, he often urged his officers never to be ashamed to take cover during heavy shelling, if cover was possible.

On one occasion I was looking over the parapet of the Front Line on a quiet sector, little thinking that our C.O. was watching me from the next fire-bay. Needless to say I never repeated the operation unnecessarily !

" On the 23rd April, 1917, accompanying the leading wave in an attack near Guémappe, our C.O. personally controlled the movements of the battalion throughout, inspiring by his presence all who took part. The attack was a great success, and resulted in the capture, with a minimum of casualties, of our objectives, together with a large number of prisoners."

But before this successful attack the 9th had been adding to their great reputation.

Early in March there were signs and rumours that the enemy contemplated retiring behind the newly prepared Hindenburg defences. Speculation was rife, and accurate knowledge of the German dispositions was of more than unusual value.

On March 4th a party of the 9th carried out a daring and successful raid in the Foucaucourt area, capturing some Prussian prisoners and gaining information that was badly needed. For two more days they remained in this sector, and then were relieved and went back into billets at Mericourt on the Somme.

In April, however, they arrived near Arras, and on the evening of April 12th, three days after the capture of Vimy Ridge, they relieved the 10th D.L.I., commanded by Lieut.-Col. (afterwards Brigadier-General) H. H. Morant, who, it will be remembered, had at one time been Roland's C.O.

General Morant has described this incident most graphically.

" Bradford's battalion came up to relieve mine after the first two days of the Battle of Arras. It was an awful night, dark as pitch, with a blizzard raging. He arrived at my dugout about midnight. After greeting me most respectfully (though we were of similar rank), and after a very brief and modest account of his recent doings in the War in answer to my inquiries, he asked me to excuse him while he issued orders to his second in command, Quarter-Master and Transport Officer. The way he gave these orders impressed me greatly. Though he had come up in the dark and in a blizzard to a perfectly strange locality, he had noted positions for cookers, transport lines and everything and everyone, and then he proceeded to give clear and brief but comprehensive orders to each one. This lad, who barely five years previously had been attached to me for preliminary training was now, unconsciously no doubt, giving me a lesson as to how things ought to be done."

In the Arras offensive the 50th Division were introduced to a type of fighting very different from that they had previously experienced. At the moment when they took up their assigned position, the advance had been carried forward some four miles, but the British troops, having assumed more or less open warfare, were not established in any system of trenches. On April 13th, for instance, the 9th D.L.I. relieved a battalion of the London Regiment, which had been occupying the bank of a sunken road in the neighbourhood of Wancourt Ridge. The position was enfiladed by the enemy from a village, but " the prompt action of the Lewis Gunners kept hostile fire down to a minimum, and no great inconvenience was suffered."

On the following day reconnoitring and fighting patrols cleared the ground for a few hundred yards forward, and when it was dusk the battalion moved up, occupied and consolidated the ground that had been gained.

In these and similar minor operations the training which the 9th had received since its reorganisation proved its value times and again. Roland had never lost sight of the fact that the stalemate conditions of trench warfare would eventually pass, and in lectures to his officers he had always emphasised the fact that " the principles which govern the attack in the open are the principles which govern almost every military operation," and he had insisted that all training should be based upon these principles.

The result was that his men could accommodate themselves easily to the new conditions, and so were able to do exceptionally valuable work.

Roland has left some rough notes, which show the system on which he worked and made his battalion so famous. They are given as they were written :

" Army same as any business concern.
Coy., Platoon & Section Commander have straightforward task—to keep Platoons & Sections in a highly efficient state.
Leadership—ability to make comrades follow you.
Within power of everyone to become a Leader.
Ability to appreciate requirements of human nature.
Some are born leaders, but all if they try can become so, and it is their duty to try.
1. Understand Human Nature.
2. Power & ability to set example to subordinates.
3. Knowledge.
4. Determination & intensity of purpose.
5. Optimistic and enthusiastic.

1. Look after men's comfort & welfare.
   Understand temperament & characteristics of
       men, prejudices.
   Men not machines.
   Justice.
   Friend as well as leader.
2. Fitness & Endurance.
   Courage.
   Cheerfulness.
   Appearance on & off.
   Bearing to all ranks."

On the principles to be found in these notes
Roland must both have acted and tried to make everyone in his battalion act.

It has been eloquently said of another great
soldier that he had an " aching affection for his regiment—the devotion of a ' lover or a child.' " With
equal truth these words might have been used of
Roland's feelings for his battalion, for he and his men
were linked together by mutual love and purpose, and
such ties as these can defy death and worse than
death—the forgetfulness that time brings with it.

CHAPTER XI.

For a few days in the latter part of April the 9th D.L.I. were resting in the caves at Ronneville. These caves were a natural protection against enemy shelling and were large enough to accommodate a whole brigade. They were fitted with electric light, and in these weird surroundings, despite some inconvenience from dampness, the men managed thoroughly to enjoy themselves. But very soon they were back in the line again.

On the 23rd of April, St. George's Day, the 150th Brigade carried a German position near Guémappe, but were forced out of it by a strong counter-attack. After this action the 9th D.L.I., at first in reserve, were ordered with little or no artillery assistance to counter-attack the Germans. Supporting each other by covering fire, companies moved forward in an action which developed into conditions undistinguishable from the open attacks of the days before trench warfare was known. In his diary Major Crouch, D.S.O., who was second in command of the 9th, has described this attack :

" By its quick delivery, led by the Colonel in the first wave, it outflanked the enemy, who immediately surrendered. This action was one of the most successful carried out by us. Having regard to the results obtained, casualties were extremely small. The line was re-established and remained firmly in our hands. We captured over 300 prisoners, two large howitzers, which the enemy had destroyed, and many machine guns, thirteen of which were serviceable. The more important work of consolidating our position prevented us from salving the whole fruits of this success, and much booty had to be left. The enemy dead were thickly strewn about the area.

" This action would have gladdened the heart of the stoutest martinet, the value of ' training, training, training ' being forced home to the most casual observer. The men, under their section, platoon or company commanders, worked as though on an ordinary practice attack."

After this successful action the 9th D.L.I. were for a short time among the selected troops which were organised to move forward in support of attacks made by other units. Then they went to St. Amand and remained there in training until June 15th, by which time it is not the smallest exaggeration to say that the battalion was as efficient as any battalion trained under such conditions can ever hope to be.

Working with unflagging energy, taking no mid-day meal because it interfered with his work, and constantly planning both pleasures for his men and also devices for defeating the enemy, Roland was at this time as happy as at any time in his career.

An officer, Major Veitch, M.C., who knew him well, has written of him: " He had an extraordinarily charming personality. His smile and greeting on meeting you actually made you feel that there was nothing he liked better than to see you. His first thought for everyone, officers or men, was their comfort. His attention to details was extraordinary. He saw to everything himself, even to superintending a working party."

Major Veitch also mentions another incident, which shows clearly the general opinion of Roland's fearlessness.

" I remember," he writes, " Lt.-Col. Hedley, who was commanding the 5th Bn. The Border Regiment, telling me that during one stage of the Battle of Arras he had had a bad time. He said that after an attack he went forward with Colonel Bradford to see the position, and that while they were moving up they got caught in a bad bout of shelling ; and his words to me were : ' When I saw that *even* Bradford was afraid I thought that it was all up with us.' "

In his determination to guard the interests of his men there is conclusive evidence that, on the subject of leave, Roland did not mince his words when speaking to those of higher rank than himself.

He was always thinking about leave for his men, and urging that more of them should be sent on leave. Things approached something in the nature of a crisis when a General paid a visit to the 9th. Without hesitation Roland tackled him on the subject of leave, and during the course of the conversation frankly stated that the leave which ought to go to the fighting troops was taken by the staff behind the lines. This remark not unnaturally caused the subsequent conversation to be more than a little animated. " For a little time," we are told, " the General eyed Bradford up and down as though he would place him under arrest," and then told him that " leave for the men was his first consideration and that the leave was properly allotted."

Roland, however, refused to be convinced, and it was perhaps fortunate that the man with whom he was dealing had a considerable knowledge of human nature and some sense of humour. For this incident ended in the General patting Roland on the back and remarking that he was damned glad someone was as interested in the men's leave as he himself was.

Unquestionably Roland in his enthusiasm ran risks of incurring displeasure in high places, but once convinced that he was right a troop of Field Marshals would not have persuaded him to the contrary.

" I must say," a fellow-officer who admired him unstintingly has written, " that he appeared rather tactless in his official letters, but his nature was well understood at Brigade and Division Head-quarters. It was always realised that he was so much wrapped up in the subject of his letters that he never considered what they would appear like to others. And even if remonstrated with he always had the courage to stick to his opinions."

It is possible to think that reckless would be a more appropriate word than tactless to use of Roland in this connection. In ordinary circumstances the best authority exists for the statement that he possessed tact to an exceptional extent. It is one of the qualities that we are told emphatically was his. But when he was placed in a position of authority and saw that certain things were not as he thought they should be he risked everything in his desire and determination to put them right.

With sound judgment he foresaw that the Germans after we had introduced Tanks would soon counter-attack with them. And so he set to work himself, and asked his officers to follow his example, to consider methods by which the German Tanks could be defeated. But this was only one of the many subjects he discussed and considered with the one object in view of beating the enemy.

With unquenchable ardour he strove his hardest to perfect his plans. No detail was too small for him to supervise, no task was too heavy for him to tackle. An address which he delivered during this period to men newly arrived from England, must be quoted in full, showing as it does how his early and rigorous training as a speaker ultimately became of great value both to himself and his men.

" Comrades," he said, " I want to welcome you all to the 9th Durham Light Infantry. Most of you will have heard something of our Battalion. It has a great reputation. That reputation is not built up by one or two flash-in-the-pan incidents. It has been built up by the hard honest work and soldierly conduct of the men at all times, and by their skill and pluck in action during a period of over two years' Active Service.

" Our Battalion is universally respected and envied, so you see a great responsibility rests with you. You have got to help us to maintain, and even increase, our present efficiency.

" You must always do the best work of which you are capable, try hard and conscientiously to keep yourselves fit, happy and efficient. Make yourselves masters of your own particular job as soldiers; do your duty willingly and thoroughly.

" The Call of Duty is a sacred one. We must do our duty, not merely to gain praise and advancement thereby, but because it is our duty, our duty to ourselves, our comrades, our Battalion, our families, our country, our King and to the God who made us, and who will help us in our work.

" You will find that you will be happy in this Battalion; you will find some splendid friends; your officers and non-commissioned officers are men who realise that they are made of the same clay as you, and are in sympathy with your difficulties, and will do all they can to look after your interests. They know their job and will lead you well at all times.

" We are all working for the same purpose, the complete defeat of the enemy, and we must work together, each for each, and all for each.

" Upon behalf of the gallant lads whom I have had the honour to command, I welcome you to our midst. You are now of us, and will work with us and for us.

" My friends, I am going to arrange for the Band to play one verse of the hymn, ' Abide with me ' every evening. I would like all of you then reverently to join in the words. It should mean more to you and me than the singing of a well-known hymn. ' Abide with me ' should be no mere catch-phrase with us.

" It means that we realise that there is Someone who really abides with us, and who will help us to help ourselves. Someone who is with us in all our sorrows and hardship, and every man in the world has a fair share of that.

" We soldiers should find great comfort in that fact, however much our comrades and those about us may overlook our work, there is Someone who sees and appreciates it. He is with us, I say, just as our friends, Sergeant Caldwell, Corporal Guy, and Private Halley are now serving with Him."

During the summer months of 1917 the 9th D.L.I. were once more engaged in a long spell of trench warfare. During this period Roland was as eager as ever to make life as endurable as possible for his men, and he kept a very strict and kindly eye on them. He insisted that they should shave regularly while in the trenches, and with his hatred of untidiness of all kinds he also insisted that such things as paper and cigarette ends should be cleared away. It was, indeed, a matter of honour with him that his men should hand over the trenches in a better condition than they had found them.

We hear of two incidents during these months that are worth telling because one of them proves how careful Roland was as regards detail, and the other shows how tender and kind he was in time of trouble.

" Reading through my Intelligence Report one day," Mr. Plummer says, " and noticing several i's not dotted, he said with characteristic frankness, ' I can't write well myself, but that is no reason why you shouldn't.' "

The second incident is of a very different nature.

" In June, 1917," Mrs. Rochester Dixon has written, " my nephew who was also my ward, Second-Lieutenant C. J. Dixon, 9th D.L.I., was killed in action, and I had word from an absolutely reliable source that Brigadier-General Bradford insisted upon digging the poor boy's grave with his own hands, although he had his full Burial Party with him. He also intended to read the Burial Service himself, but this he did not do, as at the last moment an Army Chaplain arrived and read the Service. This action of the General's seems to me, from what my nephew has written about him, as typical of the consideration which he always showed towards his juniors, and I know from a member of the Burial Party that it made a very great impression upon everyone who was present."

Such acts were quite spontaneous, and they endeared Roland to all who served under him, great though his demands were upon them.

In August he wrote to his brother George, congratulating him upon his promotion :

" Dear Georgie,

" I was very pleased to hear of your promotion to Lieut.-Commander.

" All is going well over here. There is plenty of hard fighting to be done, although adequate rest between times.

" There appears to be a great deal of peace talk at home. But I cannot believe we will be able to get the terms for which we set out until we have, at least, convinced the enemy that we can defeat his armies.

" Baby (his sister) seems to be having a good time in Ireland.

" What a pity it is that the Russians are no longer striking in concert with the other Allies.

" I hope that all is well with you.
         " Your affectionate brother,
" 25.8.17.   R. B. BRADFORD."

Roland, one feels, would have approved whole-heartedly of the address Abraham Lincoln delivered in 1865, in which he said, " With firmness in the right, as God gives us to see the right, let us stride on to finish the work we are in, to bind up the nation's wounds, to care for him who shall have borne the battle, and for his widow and his orphan—to do all which may achieve and cherish a just and lasting peace among ourselves and with all nations."

Some weeks later he wrote again to George :

" I have just returned from four days' leave in Paris. It was a pleasant period. I can now speak French passing well ! My good luck has continued. Although a C.O. now has no better chance of surviving than any of his men.

104

"The Americans I have seen have all been a keen, well-set-up body, who appreciate all we have done, and who are anxious to learn all they can.

"The morale of our soldiers is very high, and their efficiency is of an excellent standard. Our Ally Russia has indeed proved a broken reed. I suppose you have never thought of entering Parliament. There should be a great opportunity in politics after the War for an honest man to get on and do most interesting work. There would be a great public leaning towards service men, and if you did decide on such a career you might one day become 'The Ruler of the King's Navee.'

"I was interested to hear that you have pulled stroke in the two crews.

"My own condition is soft, and I fear I could not go even a couple of two-minute rounds with you. I hope to get leave in December (D.V.)."

Before this second letter was written the 9th D.L.I. had been given another opportunity to distinguish themselves, and had promptly made the most of it.

In the middle of September the Battalion was again sent to the Cherisey Sector. Trench-mortar and machine-gun strafing, and harassing artillery fire had rendered the enemy very jumpy and elusive. Constant raids had been made into the German lines, but the results had been meagre and disappointing.

A decision therefore was made to carry out an offensive operation on a much larger scale, and the task was entrusted to the 9th D.L.I.

―――――

CHAPTER XII.

An account of the raid which the 9th D.L.I. made on Sept. 15th, 1917, was afterwards officially published, and circulated among units in training as an example of how a raid should be carried out.

On that Saturday afternoon in September three companies went over the top, penetrated the enemy's second line and entered Cherisey village. The raid was admirably planned and executed with splendid artillery and trench mortar co-operation.

Dummy figures and dummy tanks were used with such success that they drew most of the enemy's fire. The raid was accompanied by a party of sappers with mobile charges, whose duty was to deal with the enemy who withdrew underground; all who refused to come out were blown up in their dugouts, and it was estimated that at least one hundred were killed in this way. About thirty prisoners and a few light machine guns were brought back.

So completely were the Germans taken by surprise that the British had entered their front line before any barrage was put down. And the natural result of this was that the casualties suffered both in going and returning were very small.

" One figure," an eye-witness of this raid has said, " stood out prominently on the parapet at zero-hour; that of our beloved Colonel, who was helping the men out of the trench. He then went forward into No Man's Land to see his boys reach their objective, and afterwards doubled back through the enemy barrage, to telephone his report to the General.

He had asked permission to lead the men over, but had been forbidden to do so. But he would not be denied the pleasure of seeing the boys enter the enemy line."

The German official report of this raid was most amusing to read. It described the use of tanks and much hand-to-hand fighting, after which the raiders were driven back.

Nothing further from the truth could be imagined. What really happened was that the enemy either ran away as fast as their legs would carry them, or took refuge in funk holes. Not a single case of hand-to-hand fighting took place. The raiders were not driven back, but, having achieved their purpose, retired without any haste whatever.

So perfect an example was this of a successful raid that the letter of Lt.-Col. H. Karslake (G.S.O. 1, 50th Division), who witnessed it, demands full quotation.

On September 17th, 1917, he wrote:

My dear Bradford,

In case it should interest you, I should like to tell you what I saw of your gallant lads on Saturday.

Almost simultaneously with the first burst of artillery fire they were swarming out of the front line.

They went forward slowly; I could see some men shooting from the hip.

Officers walked about slowly as they directed the men to the various gaps in the Boche wire. Once through that, they appeared on top of Narrow Trench. The men on the right were the first to arrive, and they immediately began to fire, from the shoulder standing up, at what I imagine were Boches running away on the left.

Very soon most of them had disappeared, but some, including an officer, spent the whole time walking up and down on top of Narrow Trench as if nothing imminent was happening.

Then about three Boches and two of our men came back towards Lone Sap, and were followed at once by two Boches and one of our men from the direction of Brown Mound.

From that direction also came what I took to be a runner carrying a board. He jumped into our own front line just short of Short Alley.

About 4.22 p.m. I saw four fellows coming back slowly; an officer, standing on the parapet at Narrow Trench, waved to them with his helmet, evidently directing them to the gap in the wire.

I only saw one man move out of a walk, and he came from the extreme left some minutes after most of the front lines had got back from the wire. He doubled along towards Byker Sap and suddenly dropped. I was afraid he was hit, but he picked himself up and got in safely, having evidently been tripped up by the wire.

I was greatly relieved to see two stretcher bearers returning with the stretchers over their shoulders. Then I left, having seen one of the finest examples of discipline that anybody could wish to see.

Please accept my sincerest congratulations.

Yours very sincerely,

H. KARSLAKE.

For several days after this successful raid the Germans gave full vent to their anger by showering every variety of projectile at our lines. But so greatly improved were our methods of holding the line that we did not suffer a single casualty from this rain of fire.

A few nights afterwards Roland organised a smaller raid, which was carried out without his men suffering any casualties, although it served its purpose in gaining the information that was required.

By the end of September the battalion were back in Divisional Reserve, with their work in the Cherisey Sector completed. Considering the strenuous nature of the calls made upon them during the six months of almost continuous activity around Arras, the number of casualties was wonderfully small.

According to the battalion records the casualties were :.

Officers.—Killed, 3; wounded, 18 (including the C.O., who, however, did not leave the line).

Other Ranks.—Killed, 26; wounded, 202; missing, 1.

Mid-October found the 50th Division back again in the Ypres salient, where they had rendered such a gallant account of themselves in April, 1915, within a fortnight of landing in France. Soon after their arrival the weather became worse than bad, and the ground was in such a condition that active operations had perforce to be abandoned.

At the beginning of November the 9th D.L.I. were holding a line of water-logged shell holes near Houthulst Forest, and on the 4th Roland was again wounded, but did not leave the line.

Of this incident an officer of his battalion has written :

" During his last visit to his battalion in their shell hole posts, before receiving news of his promotion to Brigadier-General, he had reached the extreme left post and was talking to the Company Commander when a German machine gun opened out. About the third bullet pierced the Company Commander's steel hat and the splinters from it wounded our Colonel in the face. He simply got up and said to the Company Commander, ' Are you hurt ? What an idiot I was not to get down when I heard the first shot.'

" Being satisfied that his companion was all right he walked back to get his wounds dressed."

On the following day Roland was promoted Brigadier-General to command the 186th Brigade of the 62nd Division, thus becoming at the age of twenty-five the youngest General in the British Army. Despite his wounds he refused to leave the line until relieved by the officer appointed to take over his command.

This determination of Roland's not to leave his beloved battalion until his successor had arrived was natural enough, but it caused a little peevishness in some quarters.

" Although," we are told, " notice of his appointment to command a Brigade was sent up to Lt.-Col. Bradford and he was ordered to report at Division Headquarters, two or three days passed without him putting in an appearance. Eventually the Division 'phoned the Brigade and the D.A.A.G. said, ' Where the devil is Bradford? Here have we been trying to get him a Brigade for the last six months, and now that he has got one he won't go to it !' Bradford insisted on remaining with his battalion until it was relieved, and then he left us to take up his new command. And that was the last we saw of him."

It is perfectly true that Roland was so attached to his battalion that promotion brought with it more regret than pleasure. But the only reason why he did not report himself at once was that he was waiting for his successor to come before he left the battalion.

On the 5th of November he wrote to his eldest brother, without even mentioning his wounds :

Dear Tommy,

I have been appointed a Brig.-Gen. (Temporary) to command the

186th Infantry Brigade,

B.E.F., France.

This came as a surprise.

I hope you are keeping well. For the next week or two I will be very busy. So do not expect any letter. Perhaps you will be kind enough to forward this letter to Georgie when you next write.

" Sonia " arrived last week. It should be interesting. Many thanks for it.

With best wishes,

Your affec. brother,

R. B. BRADFORD.

It is a remarkable letter when we think of the circumstances in which it was written. An unique distinction had been conferred upon Roland, but not even a trace of excitement nor gratification did he show. One cannot help recalling George Bradford's words when writing to his sister : " A quaint family i' faith, pukka Dickens' characters."

Two reasons quite obviously prevented Roland from rejoicing over his appointment : first that he was sincerely sorry to leave the men who loved him and whom he loved, secondly, that every thought of himself, except as a soldier whose duty it was to help his country, had been entirely obliterated by greater issues. The War had become in his mind a Holy War. We talked glibly during those critical years of the struggle of Right against Might, but what was to some of us at least a catch-phrase, comforting enough and exhilarating, had a deep and profound meaning to him.

Roland, we are told, never preached "Hate," and it is true, but this did not prevent him from detesting Prussianism and all that it stood for. Root and branch he wished to destroy such a menace to civilisation. And not for a moment did he underrate the strength of the enemy in the field nor underestimate the detestable idea for which they were fighting.

Two or three days after Roland had received his promotion he bid good-bye to his battalion.

"Comrades," he said, "we have endured many hardships together, and it is against my wish that I leave you, but as a soldier I must obey orders. I asked permission to stay with you until the end of the War, and no honours nor promotions can ease the ache in my heart on leaving you. When the War is over, I hope we may meet again and talk over the days when we fought together."

It was a scene intrinsically pathetic, and in the light of what was so soon to happen far more than pathetic.

"No one," an officer of the 9th D.L.I. who was present writes, "who witnessed that scene in a shell-holed field of Flanders is ever likely to forget it. The battalion was formed up to bid farewell to our hero Colonel, and he rode up and, dismounting, made a short speech. . . . He shook hands with every officer and man, and was so overcome with emotion that he was compelled to gallop away from the sight of the battalion he loved so well, thus leaving us no opportunity to express in public our gratitude to him under whom it had been so great a privilege to serve. He left behind him a battalion with a reputation second to none."

A page of history, an infinitely valuable page, was closed, and Roland having torn himself from his battalion lost no more time in taking over his new command.

His battalions were comprised of Yorkshiremen, part of the West Riding Division of Territorials. The affair at Cambrai was in preparation, and the Division was to form the centre of the attack. Hurriedly Roland was fitted out with the uniform of his new rank; a Divisional General lent him his cap, and another Brigadier contributed the crossed swords from an extra tunic.

In a brief, but stirring, speech, of which a record exists, he introduced himself to his Brigade.

" Comrades," he said, " I come to introduce myself to you as your new Brigadier. This is the first opportunity I have had to speak to you by day. I am going to ask you to put your implicit trust and confidence in me; to look upon me not only as your Brigadier but as your friend.

" By the help of God I will try to lead you to the best of my ability, and remember your interests are my interests.

" As you all know, in a few days from now we are going to attack. Your powers are going to be tested; they must not fail you.

" Above all, pray. ' More things are wrought by prayer than this world dreams of.' It is God alone who can give us victory, and bring us through this battle safely."

In his new sphere Roland made an instantaneous impression. " After a short week," we are told, " his men would have done anything for him. It was the same with the officers. He won all hearts at once; his manner of dealing with older men, who were soldiers when he was in the school-room, was charming. And yet there was never any doubt who commanded his Brigade."

Soon indeed was his Brigade to be put to the test.

On the morning of the 20th of November, before dawn, the attack began.

Silently, unheralded by any artillery barrage, the British tanks pushed forward into the mist, and the infantry followed them. Before darkness fell the 62nd Division had occupied the villages of Graincourt and Anneux, and had established a line 250 yards north of the Cambrai road. Their booty comprised 50 machine guns, two 8-inch howitzers, a battery of 5.9's, and a thousand prisoners.

The impenetrable Hindenburg line was penetrated. " The attack of the Division," said the official despatch, " constituted a brilliant achievement in which the troops concerned completed an advance of four and a half miles from their original lines, over-running two German systems of defence and gaining possession of three villages."

On the morning of the 21st the Division pushed northward into the trench of the Marquion Line, along the face of Bourlon Wood. Here they were exposed to a severe and continuous enfilade fire from machine guns south of the village, which temporarily forced them to retire. But they recaptured the position on the following day without the aid of tanks.

The 62nd Division then handed over its front to the 40th Division, but after a short rest they came back into the line and were at once called upon to make an attack upon Bourlon village and wood, simultaneously with the attack of the Guards upon Fontaine.

"I have heard the opinion expressed," Sir Percival Phillips wrote, "that this operation was worthy of even greater praise than the first push of the 20th, for the men were not so fresh. One exceptionally fine incident was the recapture of some high ground in Bourlon Wood by a detachment of Yorkshiremen led by Brigadier-General Bradford, V.C. These men took back a very strong position, wired it, and handed it over intact to the Division which relieved them."

On the night before Roland's Brigade was to make its attack on Bourlon Wood an incident occurred which once more shows how considerate he was of those he commanded.

"When on the staff of Ripon dispersal station," a soldier, who had served as a Corporal in the 9th D.L.I., writes: "I met a Wesleyan padre, who was attached to the 62nd Division in France. He told me that he had been sent for by Brigadier-General Bradford on the night before the latter took over his Brigade to the attack of Bourlon Wood. The Brigadier wanted a list of places where padres could be found during the attack, and expressed the opinion that padres during such an event were as important as any General. It was the first time, the padre told me, that such a request had been made of him."

In the briefest possible time Roland had proved himself worthy of the confidence he had asked his Brigade to place in him. After this attack his men would have followed him anywhere, for now they had seen with their own eyes that his reputation as a fine soldier and fearless man was based on grounds that were absolutely sound and true.

CHAPTER XIII.

In the subsequent fighting round Cambrai it will be remembered that the Germans, launching their counter-attack on the 30th of November, succeeded in taking from us some of our hard won gains. And it was during this fighting that, on the morning of this last day of November, Roland Bradford was killed.

During the Battle of Arras we are told that one of Roland's runners said to an officer, " We have a funny Colonel, sir. I was going to the line with him, and we came to a shell-hole with a dead Jerry in it. The Colonel stopped and then said to me, ' That is how I would like to die. Serving my country, wouldn't you?' "

Roland during these critical years had lived solely to serve his country. He had served it without stint, thoughtfully, ably, and with supreme courage. " In the hot fit of life, a tip-toe on the highest point of being, he passed at a bound to the other side."

Between nine and ten o'clock on that November morning he left the dugout without saying where he was going. Heavy shelling was taking place, and casualties were constantly occurring round the dugout during the day.

When Roland did not return it was thought at first that he had gone to visit the battalions which were stationed some little distance away. Later on, however, when he still did not come back, a search-party was sent out, but failed to find him. It was not until after mid-day that any news of him was heard, and then a note was brought in to say that he was killed. He had been hit in the back by a fragment of a shell, and mercifully his death must have been instantaneous.

In the orders of the 62nd (West Riding) Division published a day or two later his death is recorded in the following words:

" It is with the deepest regret that the Divisional Commander has to announce that Brigadier-General R. B. Bradford, V.C., M.C. (D.L.I.), commanding the 186th Infantry Brigade, was killed in action on November 30th.

" Though General Bradford has been so short a time in command of the 186th Brigade, the exploits of that Brigade in their wonderful advance on November 20th and succeeding days will ever be associated with his name, no less than will the fighting and consolidation in Bourlon Wood.

" The 62nd (West Riding) Division is the poorer by the loss of so gallant and determined a leader, and the Army can ill afford to lose a soldier of real genius such as was our late comrade.

" Walter Braithwaite,

" Maj.-General commanding 62nd Div."

Even at a time when we British were almost inured, as it were, to loss and suffering, the death of one so young and so gallant called forth immeasurable and heartfelt expressions of sorrow.

" He had only been with us a short time," an officer in his Brigade wrote at once, " but he had already endeared himself by his exceptional charm of manner to every officer and man in the Brigade. He inspired the most wonderful confidence in everyone, and the men would have gone anywhere for him. We have lost a real friend and a great leader."

117

Quotations from letters of sympathy and admiration could be given without number; but none of them, we feel quite confident, would have been dearer to Roland's heart than Lance-Corporal King's.

King had been Roland's servant from 1912 until the end, they were not only servant and master, but friends, and Roland did not forget in his will to leave a generous legacy as a remembrance for so many years' faithful service.

" The General," King wrote, " let me go on leave three days before they had to go into action on November 20th, and I got back on December 2nd. The poor General was killed on November 30th, and the first words I spoke when I got back were to some of the men of his Brigade asking if he was all right. And they gave me the sad answer, and I can tell you it nearly broke my heart after being with him so long. I have been back nearly a fortnight and can't get settled down at all; I feel as though I don't know where I want to be."

Roland had won, and had deserved to win, both affection and admiration, and at this moment men of high rank and of low alike found time in the stress of war to add their tributes to his memory.

In appreciation of Roland Mr. John Buchan wrote these touching and comforting words :

" It is customary, when we count the cost of war, to dwell especially upon the sacrifice of youth. The young men who would have shaped the future have perished in laying its foundations. Gifts of inestimable value to the world have been lost to it before they could find scope or fruition. Poets and thinkers have died, mute but not inglorious; men of action, statesmen, builders of society have passed before they could reveal themselves, leaving only an inheritance of ' unfulfilled renown.'

" But there is another side to the tragedy. There are many of the dead whom we can think of as having been born for the Great War, as having always been in training for it. Boys fresh from school or college have found in a few years of campaigning a far richer career than most men who reach the full span of life. In a short space they attain perfection, for

" ' It is not growing like a tree
In bulk, doth make man better be.'

" Who, in the retrospect, can say that lives like Francis Grenfell's or William Congreve's were not fully lived?

" Our first feeling when we hear of such losses is oft tragic waste; but our later and wiser thought is of a most complete and splendid fulfilment.

" In the long roll of the young dead Roland Bradford is in some ways the most conspicuous figure. In three years of war he had made a great career, and he fell at the age of twenty-five, the youngest General in the British Army. His family, which contained both Durham and Kentish strains, had a war record which few could equal."

He is buried in Hermies British Cemetery, near Havrincourt, France.

It has been quite impossible to write of Roland Bradford without real feelings of pride and affection. His impulsiveness and charm as a boy, his zest and eagerness for life, his affection for and eternal thoughtfulness of those who were near and dear to him, are qualities that call all the world over for love and admiration. And when the time came for him to occupy positions of great responsibility he never flinched nor faltered.

He once said, almost to himself, " What a strange thing fear is, and, that some people are more afraid than others." He seemed to be troubled and perplexed about it, and well he might be. For he himself was fearless, not only when facing the dangers of war, but also in matters that were comparatively trifling, though often harder to battle against than bigger, graver troubles.

It is true to say of him that as the years went on he became free from littleness of any kind. The War was a crusade, and he the very best type of crusader.

It has been said of another fine gentleman and soldier, General the Hon. Osbert Lumley, that: " The people under his command in the Army—and at one time it was a large command—all felt the encouragement and, when restraint was needed, the restraint of an extremely fine and noble integrity, a direct purpose and a clear mind, not clothed but penetrated with generosity, kindliness, candour. . . . He seemed to carry about carelessly an open secret of happiness and good will, to leave much of the rhetoric of life alone, and to save his powers of decision and perseverance for the real business of life, which was for him to do the best he could for everyone. He seemed to walk unaffectedly upon a high path and in the light."

No one can read this fine tribute of the Rev. P. N. Waggett's to General Lumley without realising how appropriate it also is to Roland Bradford.

Roland walked unaffectedly upon a high path and in the light, he saved his powers for the real business in hand, he was a perpetual source of encouragement to others, his purpose was direct, and that purpose was to save his country by defeating the enemy.

When Roland went to France in 1914 it would be untrue to say he was a strict disciplinarian. His platoon never failed to do admirable work, but its strength and fine fighting qualities were founded more upon friendliness and good feeling between himself and his men than upon actual discipline. When, however, he was promoted to a Company and to higher commands he realised that he could not rely upon the intimate personal feeling that was possible in a small command, and he became a very strict disciplinarian. Perfection, and nothing less than perfection, was his aim as a soldier, and he aimed at it steadily and with tremendous determination. But merciless as he was when dealing with wrong-doing and with failure that came from carelessness or slackness, he never lost his temper, and his first consideration was always for his men, however rigorously he trained them.

It was due very largely to this consideration that those who were serving under him had a profound trust in his wonderful courage and ability and also in his sense of justice. And though he did not excuse their faults, no Commander was more eager and more ready to praise them for their valour and their virtues.

Pride and sorrow frequently walked hand in hand during those years of war, and never were they more inseparably connected than in the death of Roland Bradford. Sincere, indeed, was the cry of admiration and of sympathy that went up to console, as far as words can, those to whom Roland was not only a gallant soldier but also a beloved son and brother. . . .

" Not once or twice in our rough island story
  The path of duty was the way to glory."

121

And if an epitaph is needed for Roland surely none more appropriate could be found than

" Gentlest and bravest in the battle brunt—
    The Champion of the Truth—
    He bore his manner to the very front
    Of our immortal Youth."

That a memorial should be raised in Darlington to Roland Bradford and his brothers was the natural desire of those who were proud to be associated in any way with the Bradford family.

The " General Bradford Memorial Fund " was opened and met with a ready response. And in connection with this Memorial Field-Marshal Earl Haig, G.C.B., wrote :

" I knew Bradford quite well and had personally followed his career with friendly interest for some time previous to his death. He was an officer of outstanding talent and personality ; as a Battalion and Brigade Commander exceptionally young but particularly capable. His death was a great loss to the Army, and I and all who had known or served with him deeply deplored it.

" I feel with you that a National Memorial to such a gallant officer and gentleman would be a most fitting tribute to his sterling qualities. The example of his unselfish courage and devotion to duty is, in my opinion, very worthy of being kept in continual remembrance by the Nation he died to serve."

The large sum of £3,000 was contributed to this Fund, and is to be devoted to a new Hospital in Darlington, the entrance of which will be called " The Bradford Entrance."

It is impossible to imagine a more fitting memorial to these brave and gracious brothers, for whom " Service " was always a word of supreme significance and meaning.

APPENDIX.

Lecture delivered by Brigadier-General Bradford to
his officers in 1917.

This lecture, which was taken down in short-
hand by one of those present, is so valuable in itself
and so informing as regards Roland and the thoughtfulness and thoroughness of his methods that, long
and technical as it is, it demands and deserves to be
preserved.

THE ATTACK.

1.

The world has been at one time and another
lectured upon the open attack, and I make no apology
for discussing the subject again. It is such an
important and far-reaching branch of our training
that we cannot devote too much attention to it.

When we talk of the open attack we mean the
best method known to us of getting to grips with the
enemy and of defeating him, and then of taking
advantage of that defeat. If the open attack is the
best method we know of defeating the enemy, it is
obvious that it is the most important branch of our
training, and that we cannot devote too much attention to it.

The principles that govern the open attack are
those which govern almost every military operation,
whether we are acting in trench warfare or any other
phase of fighting. Consequently it behoves each one
of us to study the open attack carefully until we have
got such a mastery of its general principles that we
can apply them intelligently to all circumstances in
whatever fighting we may be engaged. I will trace
through their course the various phases of an open
attack.

First of all we will assume that a unit is advancing along a road in column of route, or perhaps it may be in some position of assembly, five or six thousand yards behind the line.

The Commanding Officer will receive orders that he is to take a certain objective and consolidate that objective. His first step is then to assemble his Company Commanders and some of his other Commanders. Having assembled them he will describe the objective to them, and will give them all the information he can about the strength of the enemy, the method in which they are holding their trenches, the nature and strength of their artillery, whether they have been holding the position for some time, or whether they are holding a newly-occupied position.

Everything, in short, that he knows about the enemy's strength and probable acts will be explained thoroughly to his Company Commanders. He will indicate to his Commanders landmarks in the direction of the advance, such as wind-mills, if there are any, or any prominent features, houses, cottages, small hills, anything that will be a good guide during the advance and enable those making the attack to keep their proper direction. He would also point out any particular features in the country, such as sunken roads, embankments and places where troops during the advance could reorganise, and where they would probably be under cover from enemy fire.

His next step is to explain the formation which he intends to adopt when the Battalion is carrying out the attack.

In most Battalions a normal formation for open fighting has been adopted, and it is well that every single man in the Battalion should have some model fixed in his mind. Upon that model we can readily adapt our formation to suit any particular circumstances, but we must have something to work upon. In our Battalion you know we have adopted such a stereotyped normal formation, and of that I will say a few words in a moment.

When the Battalion Commander has given all his explanations to the Company Commanders, they in turn will assemble their Platoon Commanders, and will explain to them in the fullest detail all they know about the attack. When the Company Commanders have given their explanations and knowledge of the attack to the Platoon Commanders, the position must then be thoroughly explained to the N.C.O.'s and men.

In an attack one of *the* most important things which men must know is where they have to get to, and what they have to do when they do get there. They must know their objective. How constantly it happens in actual operations that the individual men, and often a large number of N.C.O.'s too, have not the least idea of the place they are intended to reach, or what action they are expected to take if they reach it. Now, how can you expect men to act intelligently and efficiently if they do not thoroughly understand the nature of the work in hand? So let us remember that what we do in our training, we shall in all probability do when we go into action.

Remember that if there is a lack of earnestness and a lack of intelligence in training, there will be a lack of efficiency and of intelligence when we endeavour to carry our operations against the enemy.

The explanations for the attack, and the details of the attack, must be made clear to all ranks. Let them thoroughly understand what formation they have got to use at all times; let them thoroughly understand what action they should take when they meet with enemy opposition; let them understand what they are to do when crossing the ground between themselves and the enemy, and what they must do when the position has been captured. Then, the men can be relied upon to act intelligently and efficiently, and should the leaders become casualties the success of the whole operation will not be jeopardised.

In a real attack, and in a practice attack too, you so often find that the leaders have everything worked up in their own minds, and then if one of them becomes a casualty and ceases to be in a position to control his men, the whole operation fails because the N.C.O.'s and other men were not perfectly clear about what they had to do.

Of course, in actual practice such detailed explanation will not always be possible. Frequently no more than a few minutes will be available for the Commanding Officer to call his Company Commanders together, show them their objective, allot it quickly, and tell them to move straight away from their position to the attack. So although we are right in expecting clear and complete explanation when time is plentiful, we must also train ourselves to act quickly on orders and to anticipate them, so that when there is little time for explanation we may be able to get on with the work straight away.

2.

When the attack begins our first move towards the enemy will be carried out under artillery fire. Then, as soon as we come under this fire, we must break into what is known as artillery formation, that is, a number of small columns, at varying intervals and distances, scattered over the front across which we have to advance.

Now, the normal formation adopted in our Battalion is this—the Battalion will usually attack on a two Company front, one Company will be in support, and one in Battalion reserve under the hands of the Commanding Officer. The frontage which would normally be allotted to a Battalion would be about 400 yards, which means that each of the leading Companies would have a frontage of about 200 yards. Each Company would attack on a front of two Platoons, with the other two in support, that means that each of the two leading Platoons would have a front of about a hundred yards.

Each Platoon when they break into artillery formation will separate into two parts, two sections will be leading and the other will follow behind, but not directly behind. What we must avoid is getting regularity into our formations when under artillery fire, because if we are in regular formation it will be easy for the enemy to range and to hit us. But if we offer the enemy an irregular formation it is most difficult for them to adapt their fuses accurately.

Well, one-half of each Platoon will be leading and the other half Platoon, that is the two sections, will be following about 250 yards behind.

You will see that the Platoons are organised in depth. The great advantage of this is that when in the later stages of the advance you come to reinforce Platoons, each Platoon will be reinforced by men of its own, who know each other, who know their leader, and are accustomed to work together.

The advance is then continued in this artillery formation without any pause; none of these columns need halt, and you should very rarely halt under artillery fire, because by halting you lay yourselves open to the full attack of that artillery fire. Whereas

127

if you keep on the move you will probably be advancing just in front of this fire, and the enemy in altering their fuses will find great difficulty in hitting any particular column as it moves forward.

Besides, by continuing to advance you maintain the fighting spirit and determination of the men; whereas, if you halt, the men lose their enthusiasm to get forward and may not recover it. Also by going forward you lower the moral of the enemy.

Advance in artillery formation until you come under effective rifle or machine gun fire from the enemy, or until you reach a position where you would be in imminent danger of coming under effective fire.

You know that, in this war, we have found by bitter experience that you must be extended in open order before you come within the danger of encountering enemy fire; that position may be 1,400 yards or less from the enemy. You cannot say exactly where it will be, but directly you come to that position, the leading column must at once open out into extended order, the men extending to five paces.

The advance then will still be in quick time, and will be continued until the leading lines reach a position at which, if they advance further, they would suffer too many casualties to justify them in moving forward. So they will lie down and wait to be reinforced. The next line will soon come up and reinforce them, and when they have gained that additional weight they will again be able to move forward. No firing from our rifles must yet take place; every round of ammunition will be required at the later stages of the attack, and it is useless to shoot until we are certain that every round fired has some effect upon the enemy. The ammunition *must* be husbanded.

Having been reinforced the line will move forward until it again finds itself suffering casualties from enemy fire, and then comes the time when the advance must be continued in fixed rushes. How far from the enemy the distance may be it is impossible to say, but we have found that from 800 to 1,000 yards is usually the distance at which the advance has to be continued by these fixed rushes.

The actual fire of the enemy will dictate the exact position. And at this period of the attack you will probably be able to begin using your rifles with great effect; and the great principles to bear in mind are these—the principle of mutual support, the principle of fire and movement; you must realise that the only manner in which sections can get forward is by the aid of your own rifles.

When one section is advancing, the other section or sections must be keeping up an effective fire upon the enemy in order to keep down their fire and, generally speaking, to unsteady them so that the advance may be continued in these quick rushes.

What Section Commanders must bear in mind is that by going forward they draw the enemy fire upon themselves, and so greatly assist the remainder of the line. As soon as a section has got forward and the men have recovered their breath the Section Commander will cause his section to fire on the enemy and to direct their fire upon the target which is causing most trouble to our advance. This target need not necessarily be straight in front, more often than not it will be obliquely either to the right or left, and Section Commanders must be very alert to direct the fire upon the target which is holding up or delaying the advance. In this movement the fire of Lewis guns will play a most important part. You know their fire corresponds to the power of about fifty rifles, and consequently the tremendous support of covering fire which they can bring to bear on the enemy will materially assist our advance.

I cannot impress too strongly upon you those principles of mutual support, of fire and movement, of co-operation, of covering fire throughout the advance. It is only by putting into practice these tremendously important principles that we shall be able to get forward.

Every man, every N.C.O., every officer must be determined to get forward, cost what it may; but he must know the safest and most expedient method of doing so, and that, as I have said, is by the aid of your own weapons. It is the only way by which we can get forward. Section Commanders, then, must be always ready to take full advantage of the covering fire of other sections. When they notice that the Lewis guns or other sections are opening an effective fire upon the enemy, they must seize the chance to work themselves forward; and directly they are down they must open fire upon the enemy and thus enable the other sections to advance. I cannot make that point too plain, even if I repeated it again and again.

Another point which Section Commanders must bear in mind is that they should always, during the advance, choose the next position to which they intend to move.

In every tract of country, across which we have to advance, suitable positions for our sections have to be found. In the country, of course, in which we have been operating for many months a large number of shell-holes are to be found, and these shell-holes are ideal positions. Indeed, you cannot get a more suitable position for a section, the men can fire effectively to the front and to both flanks, and at the same time get a good deal of cover. But whether shell-holes exist or not, there are always some small undulations, some depressions, short small banks on the side of roads, and similar places, which offer great scope for Section Commanders in choosing fire positions. The advance, then, will be continued in these section rushes until we reach some position near the enemy, probably 300-400 yards away, when we find that in spite of reinforcements we cannot move forward without beating down the enemy fire by some means. That means is by our own rifle fire and our artillery fire. Our artillery are always standing by to help us in every possible way with our advance. And this emphasises the importance of always sending back information, so that we may get the full benefit of co-operation with the artillery.

A fight with the enemy to gain superiority of fire will have begun, and not until we have gained the superiority and unsteadied the enemy will we be able to continue our advance, still probably in section rushes. In those section rushes we will go forward until we get within assaulting distance of the enemy.

3.

Assaulting distance is about fifty yards. Men cannot charge for a greater distance, and then be fit at the end of the charge for the work that still remains to be done. Now, it is impossible to say at what moment this assault will be carried out, it depends upon the circumstances of the case.

Usually the assault is initiated by some local Commander, such as the Company or Platoon Commander, or even a Section Commander. This man sees that the time is right for the assault, he sees that the enemy are weakening and beginning to waver, he notices perhaps that a small party of the enemy are retreating from their position, and so he springs up and dashes there and then to the assault, taking with him the men on both his right and left. And directly the others further to the flank see that the assault has begun, they themselves will rise and dash forward.

It is impossible to get every assault to synchronise, over a big front you cannot expect all Platoons and sections to move forward at the same time. You cannot get them together, but provided that everyone realises that he must, if success is to be gained, assault as soon as he can, there will be no difficulty in carrying out an assault under actual circumstances. . . .

When the assault has been carried out, we must at once set to work to reorganise. If the position we have captured is not under enemy shell-fire, an effort will be made there to form up a section, platoon and companies in their original formation. Before, however, that is done, parties must be told off to pursue the enemy, to harass them with our fire, and to maintain touch with them.

In battle it is extremely important not to lose touch with the enemy for a moment, nor to allow them to get away without being pursued and destroyed by the effect of our fire.

Should the position be under heavy fire from either artillery or rifles it will, of course, be impossible to reorganise in that manner; under such conditions you will have to carry out a hasty organisation in the same manner as you did during the advance.

While I am mentioning this work of reorganisation, I should like to say a little more about it. During the advance by sections we must do all we can to keep the sections intact and to prevent intermingling. . . . Under certain circumstances, however, it will be impossible to avoid the intermingling

132

of sections, and when they do intermingle, a reorganisation has got to take place. And this will be done by Section and Platoon Commanders taking to themselves the men who lie nearest to them. The only way to do this is for the Section Commander to point to some man, say a few paces from him on the left, and say, " So-and-so, you are the left-hand man of my section."

If the fire is so hot that he is unable to make himself heard, the Section Commander must by gesture give the man to understand that he is the left of his section. In the same way another man will be chosen as the right of the section, and these men must be prepared to place themselves under a new leader. They must be in sympathy with this work of reorganisation, and be on the *qui vive* to conform at once to the orders of a new Section Commander. . . .

And now let us get back to our point. After this reorganisation has taken place, and after we have pursued the enemy with our fire, our patrols will be out doing all they can to keep in touch with the enemy. As I told you before, we must watch the enemy so carefully that he will be unable to make a movement of any kind without us knowing about it.

4.

After we have captured the position you may be sure the enemy will try to regain it by launching a strong counter-attack.

First of all he will possibly launch an immediate counter-attack, and we should find little difficulty in dealing with this. But after a few hours, or perhaps a day or so afterwards, you may be sure that the Germans will make a very determined counter-attack in force; and unless we are prepared to meet it we shall most certainly lose our position; all the work we have done in gaining our objective will be thrown away, and we shall suffer heavy casualties and have to return to our original position.

Again and again this has happened in recent fighting, and if we analyse the circumstances carefully we shall see that, if the men who had gained these positions had been properly trained and determined to hold them at all costs, these set-backs need not have occurred.

Now, what have we got to do to resist the counter-attack? For we can and must resist it, and no other thought but of resisting it is permissible.

First of all we must get the best possible protection against enemy artillery fire, and we gain that by consolidating properly, by digging a deep narrow trench with good traverses, or if we are not making traverses with plenty of curve in the trench. By these means we get protection from the oblique and frontal fire of the enemy artillery and localise any shells that burst in the trench.

Every man must realise that unless he digs with might and main directly he reaches his objective, he will be unable to obtain cover from shell fire, and will eventually suffer for not working his hardest. The very lives of these men depend upon the intensity with which they dig, and remember, during our training, to drive this into the men's souls. Make them realise that their power to resist counter-attack, and their power to maintain themselves in safety under enemy shell fire rests entirely with themselves. If they are prepared to expend their energy in a sensible and able manner they can be comparatively safe.

Often the position captured by us will be a trench, and then the work of consolidation will usually consist in adapting that trench to suit ourselves, in improving the existing traverses, in reconnoitring the dug-outs and, when necessary, getting them ready for our own occupation. Should these dug-outs be facing the enemy, as they probably will be, it will be necessary to build an island traverse in front of the door of each, so that shells bursting in a trench may be prevented from going into the dug-out.

Sometimes we shall find that our final objective, if it is a trench, is so battered that it is impossible to consolidate it effectively. In such a case it will be wiser to move forward 100 yards or so, and build a new, good trench where the ground is not so badly knocked about. Then our patrols, who will, as I told you, be keeping in touch with the enemy, will be watching to see if the enemy is making an attempt to form up anywhere, and if they discover any such attempt they will at once warn you, and you will report back to the Colonel, who will arrange for the artillery to be brought to bear immediately upon the position where the enemy is forming up. But we must not trust entirely to the artillery. . . . Our rifles are the weapons that will help us most of all to beat off that counter-attack. Our rifles, our Lewis guns, our hand-grenades, our rifle-grenades.

You can see, then, how important it is that our rifles should always be fit to use, and that every man should be ready at any moment to open rapid and effective fire when the enemy begin to advance. We have nothing to fear from the enemy, however strong he may be, if we have a good trench, and are able to use our rifles, and have ammunition. And when positions have been lost the reason has often been that men have failed to realise the power of their own rifles and have not used them to the greatest effect.

We can, then, resist counter-attacks if we keep in touch with the enemy by means of our patrols, if we consolidate effectively so that we may obtain as perfect protection as possible against the enemy advances, and, the most important point of all, if every man is absolutely determined to cling to the captured position, cost what it may.

5.

The foregoing remarks refer to the open attack pure and simple, and I want you to realise that the trench to trench attack is exactly the same as the open attack except that one or two especial points require consideration. As I told you at the beginning of my remarks, all tactical military operations are entirely governed by the principles which govern the attack in the open, the principle of co-operation and so forth. The special points which require consideration in trench warfare are these.

First of all a good deal of mopping up will have to be done. You know that every trench that we cross over in our advance must be mopped up by somebody. Some parties must be told off to clear these trenches entirely of the enemy, so that the men who have advanced may be in no danger of Germans coming out of their dug-outs and opening fire on those who have advanced beyond them.

Then the training of our bombers requires careful attention. For, in trench warfare, a lot of work can be done better by bombers than by anybody else. This work includes the clearing of trenches, the establishing of blocks in particular positions, the advance along trenches and the capture of blocks held by the enemy.

Next there is the all-important principle of working right up to our barrage. In every trench to trench assault we now have a creeping barrage to assist us in our advance, and the infantry must advance right up to that barrage. The distance we can move up to a barrage is about 50 yards and we must keep right up to that distance, even if we suffer one or two casualties from our own artillery.

Lastly, in the initial parts of our advance, the distances between lines and columns will have to be reduced, because in trench warfare the enemy is able at very short notice to put down a barrage on any particular position, and as soon as he has observed that our attack has begun he will place a barrage on our jumping off trench, or just behind it, in some position which will hamper the forward movement of our troops. So we have got to get our troops beyond that line before the enemy barrage comes down, and consequently our columns must be quite close together to avoid the danger of being caught by that barrage.

But with these exceptions trench to trench attack corresponds entirely to attacks in the open. In every attack you have been in or have heard of you will remember that at one stage or another they have corresponded to the stages of the open attack. . . . And all movements in trench warfare are carried out in exactly the same manner as in open warfare.

There is only one way of moving under fire, and that is, as I have told you, by mutual support of your own weapons, and that principle holds good just as much in trench fighting as in any other kind of fighting. So do not get hold of the idea that trench to trench attacks are a thing apart. They are not. If you can carry out efficiently the attack in the open, you will have far less difficulty in carrying out trench warfare of all kinds.

6.

Let me say a few words on morale. What do I mean by morale? Morale is the spirit which compels all men to do their best in all operations. It is the spirit which gives them complete confidence in the success of their own arms, complete confidence in themselves and in their leaders, confidence that they may win through, that they have the upper hand of the enemy, that man for man they are superior.

During the middle of the Verdun fighting, in the early part of last year, General Joffre issued a message to his men, in which he said : " As long as the spirit of you French soldiers is what it is, I have absolutely no fear that the enemy will ever. be able to break through." You see that he referred neither to guns nor rifles, but only to the spirit of the men, their morale. He knew that as long as their morale was what it was, no forces, be they ever so strong, would be able to break through. It must be the same with us. . . . We must have complete confidence in ourselves. And how can we gain that confidence? By careful study of our profession so that we can make ourselves one with it, and by earnest application to our training.

If we can handle our men skilfully during training they will realise that we shall lead them skilfully and well when we lead them into action. They will have complete confidence in us, and we in our turn will have complete confidence in them. And unless this is so, however strong in artillery and numbers we may be, there is not the smallest hope that we shall meet with any continuous success.

That is all I am going to tell you about the attack now . . . but you must study this subject carefully in your spare time, you must think over these general principles and not learn them off by heart, you must study them so that when you go into action you will be able to apply them intelligently, and be able to adapt them to any circumstances in which you find yourselves. And I appeal to you to put into your training such a spirit of earnestness and conscientiousness that you will inspire the men under you with the same spirit of zeal. In this way we shall be able to take full advantage of our training, and be able to realise the reason for all our formations and for all our actions, and the men will be able to use their intelligence under all circumstances and work in complete sympathy with their leaders.

If we can only make ourselves perfect in our practice attacks and operations during training, we shall, as I have told you very often, be able to carry out our operations perfectly when we come under fire.

7.

My friends, I want to conclude by telling you how proud I am to be your Commanding Officer. The success of the operation in which we have just taken part was due entirely to your personal qualities, to your ability as soldiers, and to your noble courage. It was a most difficult operation. You were called upon at short notice to move across difficult country under very trying conditions. You, however, did everything in such a soldierly manner that we were not only able to do that but also to go through the attack quite successfully, and to take a large number of prisoners with very little loss to ourselves.

This attack of ours entirely justified our past training and proved it to be right. The principles which we had been studying, the principles which we had believed to be correct, were proved in these operations to be right; and that is very inspiriting.

It proved also that the reason of our success was the fact that you in your past training had earnestly applied yourselves to your work, and had done all in your power to make yourselves, under all circumstances, capable and efficient soldiers.

IN MEMORIAM, ROLAND B. BRADFORD.

Hebrews xi. 27.

Preached in ST. CUTHBERT'S, DARLINGTON, on the 6th Sunday after Trinity, July 19th, 1925, at the unveiling and dedication of a Monument to the Memory of

ROLAND BRADFORD, V.C.,
by
HERBERT HENSLEY HENSON, D.D.,
Lord Bishop of Durham.

He endured, as seeing Him Who is invisible. Hebrews xi. 27.

1. In this sentence the sacred writer gives the secret of every genuinely heroic career, and I choose it for the text of a very short sermon on this occasion, when we are recalling with pride and thankfulness the brief but memorable career of a hero. Perhaps, of all the sacrifices which the Great War involved, the sternest and most heart-rending was the sacrifice of human promise. We saw with delight and exultation the first disclosures of individual power, and then the curtain fell. " A pitiless arrow of death " cut short the life which carried so rich a freight of hopes. " The economy of Heaven is dark," and we can see but a very little way. Appearances are as misleading

as they are seemingly conclusive. *" There are first that shall be last, and last that shall be first."* Life as we see it on earth is deeply wrapped in a cloak of paradox.

> Great is the facile conqueror;
> Yet haply he, who, wounded sore,
> Breathless, unhorsed, all covered o'er
> With blood and sweat,
> Sinks foiled, but fighting evermore—
> Is greater yet.

Who shall measure the results of such a career as ROLAND BRADFORD'S? Is it not true of him also that *" He being dead yet speaketh "*?

As we look back on that terrific crisis of the War, and with the garnered knowledge of the years estimate its cost and its consequences, do we not thank GOD for the touches of chivalry and sacrifice which shine out of the record like stars in a night of gloom? War, we know, is an apocalypse of all that is basest in human nature. If we were compelled to see it in its unrelieved horror, our faith in goodness might fail, and we might even fall into the abyss of a cynical despair. But when, against the grim background of War, we can see ever the luminous figures of those who, through its cruellest strain, and in the deepest night of its enormous wickedness, " did out the duty " in sheer nobleness of self-surrendering service, we can look up and say again our Creed of Self-respect and Eternal Hope.

The young man, whose name and fame will be perpetuated by the monument which we have dedicated in this glorious church, came on to the scene of life richly gifted with the proved constituents of the best human quality. Born of a sound English stock, reared in a home of the best type of English homes,

141

brought up in circumstances eminently favourable to the development of his powers of body, mind, and character, one of a noble band of like-minded brothers, ROLAND BRADFORD was ready when the crisis of War broke suddenly on the world, and brought to him as to his contemporaries the supreme opportunity of life. He was able to rise to the call of that great moment, and to answer triumphantly to its demands.

War is a bitter experience, a time of sifting, a purgatory of fire to the peoples. Empires sink in its flame, and empires rise. On its stricken fields the controversies of ages are brought to final arbitrament, and the courses of the future are determined in an hour. The historian traces, by the long labour of research, the causes and the consequences of the conflicts which at intervals waste the world. Something is learned, much is forgotten, much was never suspected. In the Books of GOD, the Eternal Judge, and in those books alone, the truth is written. What is true of nations is not less true of individuals. For every citizen at home as well as for every soldier on service the War meant probation, disclosure, and decision. Men disclosed the quality of their past lives, lifted the veil which shrouds personal life, and revealed the metal of character. In its stern experiences they fulfilled or disappointed the purpose of their CREATOR. " *God proved them, and found them worthy of Himself* " is the record of the Saints, and that Divine Judgment, accomplished in every life, is thrown into terrible distinctness by the swift and sudden fortunes of War. Heroes are discovered, and cowards are unmasked. It is the " *Day of the Lord,*" wherein the word of the prophet is accomplished, and " *The idols pass utterly away.*"

The quality of a man's religion is put to the proof in the strange and dreadful experiences of War.

In time of peace we take our beliefs for granted, and are satisfied with the shibboleths of religious fashion. But it is otherwise in time of War. Then the solemn accustomed phrases are too often found to be empty of meaning, and the conventions which had seemed so sound and strong, break down and pass from mind. It is as the LORD said. In the onset of the flood, and the beating of the tempest, only the house that is builded on the Rock can stand. ROLAND BRADFORD's religion stood the test of War. He belongs to the great company of Christian soldiers, men who read their dreadful duty as part of CHRIST's claim on them, and carried into the campaign the high passion of the Crusader. What a company it is! GODFRY DE BOUILLON, ST. LOUIS, SIMON DE MONTFORT, SIR PHILIP SIDNEY, GUSTAVUS ADOLPHUS, OLIVER CROMWELL, COLONEL GARDINER, and countless more —to this glorious fellowship of dedicated warriors ROLAND BRADFORD belongs. Of them severally the text might be spoken, " *He endured as seeing Him Who is invisible.*" They saw, above and beyond the diplomacy of the statesmen and the strategy of the commanders, a Plan and a Purpose which were not earth-born and earth-bound. The eternal warfare of Justice against Oppression, of Truth against Falsehood, of Freedom against Tyranny—that warfare of the Spirit which fills history with martyrdoms, and clothes human lives with unworldly splendour, was seen to be actually proceeding, and calling them. They " *Came to the help of the Lord against the mighty.*" In this transfiguring vision their warfare became selfless and sublime. It rose out of the squalor and anguish of the actual campaign, and linked itself on with the unseen things of eternity. It is the peculiar grace of Religion that it exalts, strengthens, and transforms whatever human activity it binds into itself. Common things take on a majesty which is more than regal. Authority becomes pastorate : and obedience a spiritual franchise when related to HIM " Whose service is perfect freedom." Now, of this grace of genuine Religion Soldierhood is perhaps the supreme illustration, the more notable because apart from it Soldierhood may fall into great deeps of degradation. The Christian Soldier is its noblest expression. THOMAS FULLER was drawing from life when he wrote his description of the religious warrior :

> " None fitter to go to war, than those who have made their peace with God in Christ. For such a man's soul is an impregnable fort. It cannot be scaled with ladders, for it reacheth up to heaven ; nor be broken by batteries, for it is walled with brass ; nor undermined by pioneers, for he is founded on a rock ; nor betrayed by treason, for faith itself keeps it ; nor be burnt by grenadoes, for he can quench the fiery darts of the devil ; nor be forced by famine, for ' a good conscience is a continual feast.' "

v. " *The Holy State*," p. 113.

Some rough notes on a commanding officer's duty which were found among his papers give the secret of ROLAND BRADFORD'S remarkable influence over the men whom he commanded.

" Leadership," he says, " is ability to make comrades follow you." He was right. That is as Leadership is understood by HIM, the Captain of the LORD'S Host, whose " soldiers and servants " we are. CHRIST'S formula of command is " *Follow Me*," and all authority exercised in CHRIST'S spirit must conform to HIS example.

Do you wonder why his men loved him, and obeyed him with alacrity, when you know what were

144

the notes of his leadership? Here they are set out shortly by himself:

Look after men's comfort and welfare.
Understand temperament and characteristics of men, prejudices.
Men not machines.
Justice.
Friend as well as leader.

Seen in daily relation to this version of leadership, his men found their commander's emphasis on religion very natural, nay, inevitable. When he called them together at the close of the day to sing his favourite hymn, "Abide with me," they could not mistake the meaning or fitness of the action. They divined the secret of his power, and the source of his buoyancy and cheerfulness. They would not have described it in the same words, but they would not have failed to understand the fitness of the sacred writer's picture of a Hero of Faith. Like MOSES in the dangers and temptations of Eygpt, so ROLAND BRADFORD in the stress and strain of his warfare *" Endured as seeing Him Who is invisible."*

What SHELLEY wrote of a famous Christian Soldier in an earlier age, who also died in conflict with a cruel and tyrannous oppressor, fighting in the exaltation of a spiritual conflict, may be applied to him; ROLAND BRADFORD looked on the War with Germany as SIDNEY looked on the War with Spain. They were men of the same spirit.

SIDNEY as he fought
And as he fell, and as he lived and loved
Sublimely mild, a spirit without spot.

While then we mourn, and must ever mourn, for the eclipse of this bright spirit in the early splendour of its powers, we cannot let sorrow be the prevailing mood in which we recall him here. We thank GOD for what, in his short life, he did, and still more for what he was. His memory remains to us, a precious and indestructible possession. In this town, with which he was so closely connected, his name will be treasured as a part of the civic heritage into which a citizen of DARLINGTON is born. In the difficult times through which we are passing, through the formidable dangers which are in front of us, we shall carry ourselves more manfully by the recollection of his example. Life is often called a battle, and not unfitly, for there also the pageant of moral conflict is unfolded, and men meet diverse fates. The Battle of Life calls for the same qualities as those which have touched with spiritual beauty even the violences and horrors of historic War, and which were exhibited in such fulness in ROLAND BRADFORD. Here, in this sacred place, we, the Soldiers of the Cross, take again our pledge to " *Fight the good fight* " to which in our Baptism we were pledged.

From that Monument we shall hear the summons—" *Suffer hardship with Me as good Soldiers of Jesus Christ.*" The conflict is the same, and the secret of victory is still the same.

" *The things that are seen are temporal; the things that are not seen are eternal.*" Only the Vision of the Unseen can give us mastery of the world. We, too, must " *Endure as seeing Him Who is invisible.*" In the strength of that Vision we rise above the noise and dust of conflict, " *The strife of men and the tumult of the city,*" and lay firm hold on the Changeless and Abiding.

" *For the world passeth away and the lust thereof, but he that doeth the will of God abideth for ever.*"